WATER
FOR THE
WAY

A LENTEN DEVOTIONAL

10 9 8 7 6 5 4 3 2 1

CONTENTS

DAY 1
ASH WEDNESDAY
THE FAST THAT I CHOOSE

SCRIPTURE

ISAIAH 58:1–12

Is not this the fast that I choose: to loose the bonds of injustice, to undo the thongs of the yoke, to let the oppressed go free, and to break every yoke? Is it not to share your bread with the hungry, and bring the homeless poor into your house; when you see the naked, to cover them, and not to hide yourself from your own kin? Then your light shall break forth like the dawn, and your healing shall spring up quickly; your vindicator shall go before you, the glory of the Lord shall be your rear guard.

—ISAIAH 58:6–8

Most of us, when we think about fasting, do not usually imagine ourselves as fasting for others. The usual emphasis is on personal piety. Fasting usually brings with it unannounced benefits for one's body and a healthier self—unannounced because most do not want to be seen as self-centred.

In today's scripture, Isaiah hears God's perspective on true religion, spirituality, and personal piety in and through the fasting season. Simply stated, a fast is not about starving the body. A fast is about feeding the soul. God points out that the people who have expressed publicly their desire to draw closer to God actually are rebellious and are not practicing the ways of God. Their ways are selfish and self-benefiting.

A religion that centers only on personal well-being is of no consequence in the greater redeeming purposes of God and the work of the kingdom of Christ in the world. When contrasted to the forty days of Jesus's fast in the wilderness, modern religion with its weight of self-focused practice can sometimes feel empty. Ultimately, we should be choosing the kind of fast that, as Isaiah 58:6 suggests, looses the bonds of injustice, undoes the thongs of the yoke, lets the oppressed go free, and breaks every yoke.

In some cultures, fasting sages and monks go into villages to beg for food. In doing so, their religion and sacrifice are seen by many, and they are respected for their personal spirituality. But this is not the true and right practice of the people of God. Our fasting and our sacrifices are not meant to be seen by others. Jesus instructs us in Matthew's Gospel: "And whenever you fast, do not look dismal, like the hypocrites, for they disfigure their faces so as to show others that they are fasting. Truly I tell you, they have received their reward" (6:16).

The essence of fasting is to joyfully give ourselves to others for their hunger pangs to be quenched. We are invited to fast, and perhaps even to share from our resources while we fast, so that others may feel warmth and wellness without guilt or shame. We do not fast to *show* our wealth; we fast to *share* our wealth. The generous giving of oneself is the kind of practice that reflects the image of the God of Scripture, who made the ultimate sacrifice for us so that we may be redeemed and restored.

QUESTIONS FOR REFLECTION OR DISCUSSION

1. What is your definition of true religion?

_____

_____

_____

_____

2. What are some ways we could fast that could truly benefit others?

_____

_____

_____

_____

3. If all the people of God who were able to practiced regular fasting each week, and not just during Lent, how might that positively impact the environment?

_____

_____

_____

PRAYER

Our Father in heaven, please remind us each day that it is not ritual, religious practices and repetitive words and deeds that impress you. Inspire us once again to see the point of selflessly imitating your ways in all our days. Make us more like you through Jesus our Lord's victory on the cross. Amen.

DAY 2
THURSDAY
SUSTAIN IN ME A WILLING SPIRIT

SCRIPTURE

PSALM 51:1–17

Let me hear joy and gladness; let the bones that you have crushed rejoice.
Hide your face from my sins, and blot out all my iniquities. Create in me
a clean heart, O God, and put a new and right spirit within me.
Do not cast me away from your presence, and do not take your
holy spirit from me. Restore to me the joy of your salvation,
and sustain in me a willing spirit.

—PSALM 51:8–12

Lent is a season of deep reflection, but it ought not be a season of regret and hurt. We are to embark on a journey of grace, allowing the Great Physician to give us the all clear. In 2010, my wife, MaryAnn, got to run her first ultra-marathon. The Comrades Marathon is 89 kilometres (or 55.3 miles) of grueling uphills and harsh downhills. The race must be accomplished in an allotted time of 11 hours. During her training, Mary sustained a knee injury. The experienced sports physician recommended she follow certain specific exercises, diet guides, and other suggestions he offered to strengthen the tendons in her knee. It would have been a brutal journey had Mary neglected to take the doctor's advice. One cannot go a very great distance on an injured leg.

Reading through Psalm 51, what comes to mind is a person embarking on a long journey with an injured or broken leg. The pain of a broken limb or a crushed bone is slight when compared to the desperation of the pain the psalmist expresses in today's scripture. In this psalm, David is deeply remorseful over his broken relationship with God. His song of brokenness forces one to think that a journey through this life is nearly impossible if we are to attempt it from the starting line while living in broken relationship with God.

The psalmist suggests that his broken bones must rejoice in their mended state. Sin as rebellion tends to feel like a broken bone or dislocated joint. Sin damages or severs our relationship with God. But God has made a way to heal us on the journey. Jesus is our healing ointment. By faith, when we trust that God has provided a way in Christ, we find health and help in our brokenness and pain. The brokenness on the cross brings us to identify with Jesus. We understand our own rejection and lost state when we hear the cry of dereliction, "My God, my God, why have you forsaken me?" In the resurrection and the empty tomb, though, we are filled with hope and become alive in Christ to renewed hope and rejoicing bones. We are made fit and fixed *on* the journey, not *for* the journey. God in Christ loves each person, and this love overcomes shame and guilt by restoring us when we apply belief in Christ.

QUESTIONS FOR REFLECTION OR DISCUSSION

1. What are somethings in your life that have crushed your spirit and brought you to a state of dislocation from God?

   _____

   _____

   _____

   _____

2. How do you feel about the cry of Jesus from the cross when he said, "My God, my God, why have you forsaken me?"

   _____

   _____

   _____

   _____

3. What are some ways we may prepare for the journey of life in our daily practices?

   _____

   _____

   _____

   _____

PRAYER

*Our God and loving Saviour, rescue us when we fall down.
When the weight of sin, guilt, and shame make us feel like our lives are
disjointed and disconnected from your original design for us, pour out
your wholeness on us, that we may experience your restoring,
healing grace. We want to live in your completion, in your peace,
in your holiness each day. Amen.*

DAY 3
FRIDAY
NOW IS THE ACCEPTABLE TIME

SCRIPTURE

2 CORINTHIANS 5:20–6:10

So we are ambassadors for Christ, since God is making his appeal through us; we entreat you on behalf of Christ, be reconciled to God. For our sake he made him to be sin who knew no sin, so that in him we might become the righteousness of God. As we work together with him, we urge you also not to accept the grace of God in vain. For he says, "At an acceptable time I have listened to you, and on a day of salvation I have helped you." See, now is the acceptable time; see, now is the day of salvation!

—*2 CORINTHIANS 5:20–6:2*

Lent is a time for deep drinking of all that will heal and make us whole. God's grace is cool refreshing water for the way. As Paul addresses the Corinthian church on the subject of reconciliation, we must be mindful that the context reflects a faith community that is at war with one another. There arose many moral and spiritual disputes. The first of the two Corinthian documents that have been handed down to us reflects contentious issues in a church divided individually and factionally. Second Corinthians reveals a church standing divided against Paul because he has taken disciplinary measures on a moral issue that has left people criticising Paul's leadership and questioning his authority as an apostle. Brokenness from strife and unforgiveness leave us thirsty for times of refreshing. The Corinthian people are murmuring against the leader, thirsty for spiritual refreshment and healing.

The imagery casts our minds back to the wilderness wanderings of the Israelites and their discomfort on the journey because of division and strife. In 2 Corinthians 6, Paul reminds the church of the words in Leviticus and Exodus where God desired to embrace the divided people again as their God, and they would again be his people. The thirst for reconciliation is only satisfied with living waters. The wells of living water must be dug out now. We cannot dig wells when we are thirsty.

We are invited to source the water now, hydrating our spirits before the days of thirst come upon us. The proclamation that "now is the day of salvation" reminds us to drink deeply and to be spiritually hydrated, saved, and healed. In the days when we are tempted to be at war with one another, let us remember that we drink from the same pools because we are on the same path. Our journey is helped when we are reconciled to each other in Christ. We are saved from the possibility of hate and the resulting hurt when we receive and accept the grace of God at the right time. To dig a well only when we sense a thirst building may be convenient, but it is not helpful. To dig the well and stay hydrated before we even become thirsty is prevenient and life-saving. Now is that acceptable time. Drink from the fountain of living water.

QUESTIONS FOR REFLECTION OR DISCUSSION

1. We tend to ignore God when life is going well. Only when we
    are in the struggle for our very existence do many of us think of
    seeking God. "See, now is the acceptable time; see, now is the day
    of salvation!" What do these words of Paul mean to you?

    _____

    _____

    _____

    _____

    _____

2. Why do we usually turn to God in the midst of strife and hurt?
    Why are we often tempted to seek convenient solutions? Does it
    not make sense to seek out the water before we become thirsty?

    _____

    _____

    _____

    _____

    _____

    _____

PRAYER

*Our Lord and our God, teach us that there is no time like the present.
Now is when we need your love and grace. Fill us with your peace and
your Spirit so that, in the days of strife and hurt, we will respond with the
abundance of living waters through Christ Jesus. May we be
life-giving streams in a time of thirst and drought. Amen.*

DAY 4
SATURDAY
PRACTICING YOUR PIETY

SCRIPTURE

MATTHEW 6:1-6, 16-21

Beware of practicing your piety before others in order to be seen by them; for then you have no reward from your Father in heaven. So whenever you give alms, do not sound a trumpet before you, as the hypocrites do in the synagogues and in the streets, so that they may be praised by others. Truly I tell you, they have received their reward. But when you give alms, do not let your left hand know what your right hand is doing, so that your alms may be done in secret; and your Father who sees in secret will reward you.

—MATTHEW 6:1-4

I love the motto of my alma mater. It is deep and cuts to the point. It simply says: *Esse Quam Videri*. It means "to be rather than to seem."

Impressing people is such a futile and tiring exercise. It is even more regretful when one thinks about the many hours we are tempted to spend impressing people with our smarts, our acquisitions, or anything else we believe tells the world, "I have arrived." The reality hits home when we realize the dead are quickly forgotten. This realization helps us understand what a waste of time it is to invest so much energy in impressing others. People quickly forget the last impressive celebrity and go on to replace the crumbling idol on the pedestal with another.

Our investments in prayer, the giving of alms, fasting, and other spiritual disciplines are futile if we only do them in order to be noticed by others. Spiritual disciplines are *relationship* practices that deepen intimacy between God and ourselves. The life lived for God's glory, poured out in a self-emptying way, is not a public show for the applause of the cheering crowds. If public praise is one's motivator, then Jesus confirms in today's scripture that public praise will be one's only reward.

The scene described in today's Gospel scripture is one where street performers blast their trumpets in order to gather a crowd. The *hupokrites*—actors—stage a performance for the entertainment of the crowds. When the show is over, the characters are folded away along with the script, and the people called the actors—the *hypokrites*—are understood to be separate from the characters they have embodied onstage.

Jesus uses the word "hypocrite" in this passage to communicate that the people of God should not be acting for public praise or benefit. The life of a Jesus follower should not be one of staged performances. Jesus is no actor! To the very last moment of his life, he lives out God's mission as a flesh-and-blood person working to redeem the broken and the lost. May our good works of secret piety and righteousness build intimacy between the Lord and his followers.

QUESTIONS FOR REFLECTION OR DISCUSSION

1. What are some ways in which people create a life that seems impressive?

   _____

   _____

   _____

   _____

2. What ought we to be to others by way of our Christlike nature?

   _____

   _____

   _____

   _____

3. How might our care and love for the people around us communicate the gospel more effectively than our public shows of piety?

   _____

   _____

   _____

   _____

PRAYER

Gracious Lord of light and love, shine through us from heaven above.
May all our neighbours, far and near, know your love and lose all fear.
May our lives in you not be an act; but to your cross, the lost attract.
Authentic lives we desire to live. All of us to you we give.
Amen.

FIRST
SUNDAY
IN LENT

DID GOD SAY . . . ?

SCRIPTURE

GENESIS 2:15–17; 3:1–7

Now the serpent was more crafty than any other wild animal that
the Lord God had made. He said to the woman, "Did God say,
'You shall not eat from any tree in the garden'?"

—*GENESIS 3:1*

Satan's strategy is to get you to love yourself and only yourself. He does this so you remain as fallen as Adam and Eve. He uses the strategy of encouraging disobedience to God, which results in being disconnected from God. His *modus operandi* is to draw our attention constantly to ourselves. Scripture testifies to this truth: "For everything in the world—the lust of the flesh, the lust of the eyes, and the pride of life—comes not from the Father but from the world" (1 John 2:16, NIV). In the garden of Eden, Satan tempts Adam and Eve with desire. In the wilderness, he tempts Jesus with the same strategy of self-centredness (see Matthew 4). And he uses the same artifices to tempt us today.

The truth is that the devil is not after our jobs or our homes or any material thing. He simply wants us to move away from an intimate relationship with God. The great enemy of our souls does not tell a lie in the garden. That's not his style. You'd be hard-pressed to find a clear passage in Scripture where Satan can be proven to be telling a lie. He does not tell lies in the Bible. He simply questions the truth. *Did God really say that?* That's how Satan destroys relationships. He questions truth and makes the truth teller the liar. *You shall surely not die.* He destabilises the one foundation upon which intimacy with God is built—trust. He speaks deceitfully, hiding the whole truth.

In all reality, Satan brings spiritual death by creating another object to trust in: a golden calf, altars in high places, the very thing we go to bed thinking about and the first thing we wake up thinking about. What the devil desires is to corrupt our ability to love God with our entire being. Our enemy works against our trust and our love. Satan questions, and encourages us to question, the very things that build commitment and dedication to God.

QUESTIONS FOR REFLECTION OR DISCUSSION

1. How do you trust God with the essence of your entire being?

_____

_____

_____

_____

_____

2. How do you trust God with your loved ones?

_____

_____

_____

_____

3. How do you trust God with your enemies?

_____

_____

_____

_____

_____

PRAYER

We trust you, Lord—you who hold our future and our past together in love. We believe you intend no evil toward us and that your thoughts about us outnumber all the stars in the galaxies and the grains of sand on the beaches. You, O Lord, have started our journey with us, and it is a journey of truth and trust, and it will end in life everlasting. Amen.

DAY 5
MONDAY
I WILL CONFESS

SCRIPTURE

PSALM 32

Happy are those whose transgression is forgiven, whose sin is covered.
While I kept silence, my body wasted away through
my groaning all day long.
Then I acknowledged my sin to you, and I did not hide my iniquity;
I said, "I will confess my transgressions to the Lord," and
you forgave the guilt of my sin.
You are a hiding place for me; you preserve me from trouble;
you surround me with glad cries of deliverance.
Many are the torments of the wicked, but steadfast love
surrounds those who trust in the Lord.

—PSALM 32:1, 3, 5, 7, 10

In 2002 at an airport in Miami, Florida, I was detained by law enforcement with a few of my African colleagues. We were in transit to a theology conference. Our transgression? We were TWOVs. The first time I heard the acronym, it sounded as though we were being called "trolls." Upon asking for clarification, we came to understand that we were classified as "travelling without official visas," and we were not allowed to continue on our trip. They threatened us with a speedy return to our point of origin, but after thirty-six hours of isolation and repeating our stories to multiple different people wearing badges, they finally confirmed we were telling the truth about being church leaders en route to a conference, and we were released.

In today's scripture, the psalmist sings the song of the blessed people who have held nothing back by way of confession to God; as a result, confessional people are freed. Transgressions and sins, according to the ancient songwriter, are the very acts of crossing the line and overstepping the boundaries of intimacy in relationship with the Source of creation. Transgressions bind people, making them no longer free. The longer we remain silent, the more our relationship with God remains stagnant—without progression or regression—and we are not free to go forward. Stagnant, we become sick unto death. The psalmist points out that there is silence, yet there is groaning. The silencing of humility kills the spirit. To withhold conversation is one thing, but to hold back confession is a prideful act that leads to sickness and, ultimately, death.

But oh, what a moment of relief when we confess and are forgiven! The river of life flows again. Creativity courses through us, and life flows in relationship. Guilt and shame are forgiven. In confession to the Creator, who we are is restored, and what we have done is remembered no more because we are forgiven and talking intimately with God again. Love and trust are restored.

QUESTIONS FOR REFLECTION OR DISCUSSION

1. What comes to mind when you think of the word "transgression?"

2. What comes to mind when you think of the word "stagnation?"

3. How has confession in prayer helped you develop your relationship with God?

4. How may we invite honest, intimate conversations in the Holy Spirit?

PRAYER

Lord, reign supremely in our lives. We open our hearts to you in spirit and truth. We bring ourselves in obedience and ask that your Holy Spirit would align our desires with the desires of God our Creator and Christ our Lord and Saviour. Cleanse our lives of selfish desires and fill us with more and more love for you. Amen.

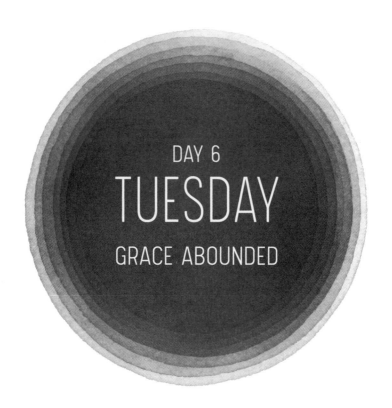

DAY 6
TUESDAY
GRACE ABOUNDED

SCRIPTURE

ROMANS 5:12–21

Sin was indeed in the world before the law, but sin is not reckoned when there is no law. But law came in, with the result that the trespass multiplied; but where sin increased, grace abounded all the more, so that, just as sin exercised dominion in death, so grace might also exercise dominion through justification leading to eternal life through Jesus Christ our Lord.

—ROMANS 5:13, 20–21

The susceptibility of all humans to the severe acute respiratory syndrome (SARS) virus was first confirmed around the turn of the century (2002). There are many viruses in the world, but humankind is not always a good host. Our susceptibility factor is what makes a virus a threat.

Likewise, the ancients who perceived the ways of God and the existence of evil saw evil as chaos. Many evils (things that cause chaos) exist in the world, but the use of particular forms of evil is what makes it sinful. Fire, water, explosives, viruses, and more all have the capacity to wreak havoc and chaos. When, for example, someone throws another person into a fire, the sum total of that evil intention is manifested as a sinful act that violates God's love in the world. When we use evil to serve the selfish advancement of the human ego, sin prevails as rebellion against God's love. Evil is exposed in conjunction with the sinful intent of the human heart.

In Romans 5, Paul says that sin existed in the world but was not "reckoned" before the law came. The term translated "reckon" is an accounting term used to describe totalling up the cost. These actions, when revealed by the light of the knowledge of God, become the very things we must count as sins. When God provides the guiding directives for humankind's best quality of life and calls it the law, it is as though the curtains in an old, dusty room have been drawn apart ever so slightly. The law is like the sunlight that seeps into the room, revealing the particles of dust in the air. The dust was already in the room. The sunlight merely reveals the presence of dust and brings it into focus. When the light of God's law breaks in, the dust of sin can be identified, qualified, and even quantified. The light, however, does not clean the room or remove the dust. Only a cleansing agent can do that.

To illustrate it another way, the law of God, as James says, is like a mirror (James 1:23). The mirror reveals the unwashed face and the degree to which the face ought to be cleansed, but the mirror is not the cleansing agent. The law brings into focus the immensity of sin and our muddied image, but only the blood of Jesus cleanses us, returning us to presentability at the dining table of the Father.

QUESTIONS FOR REFLECTION OR DISCUSSION

1. In what ways have we become infected by the use of havoc-wreaking powers? How have we harnessed destructive powers to satisfy the desires of our pride?

_____

_____

_____

_____

_____

2. How may we allow the light of God's Word, or law, to reveal the presence of sin in our darkened lives?

_____

_____

_____

_____

_____

PRAYER

Lord, allow us to see ourselves as we truly stand in the light of your Word. Lord, when we see the state of ourselves—where we are and where you desire us to be—open our hearts to the cleansing work of the Holy Spirit. Confessing that we know where much of the dust is, is not the same as being cleansed of the dust. Move us from confessing our sin to correcting our sin. Amen.

DAY 7
WEDNESDAY
LIFE FOR ALL

SCRIPTURE

ROMANS 5:12–21

Therefore, just as sin came into the world through one man, and death came through sin, and so death spread to all because all have sinned. Therefore just as one man's trespass led to condemnation for all, so one man's act of righteousness leads to justification and life for all.

—ROMANS 5:12, 18

In our reading today, we look again at this very meaty portion of Scripture. It is intense in flavour and thick with substance, and every believer must sink their teeth into this portion of God's Word. It is a passage that shows us the intersection between Adam and Christ. The passage addresses the act of Adam's transgression answered (or resolved) by the act of Christ's righteousness. We find ourselves examining Adam's selfishness in contrast with Christ's selflessness. We see Adam's condemnation, curse, and death juxtaposed with Christ's justification, promise, and life. Humankind, through Adam and Eve, destroyed the relationship between humanity and God, but God can be trusted to restore it. The action of Adam necessitated the action of Christ.

Jesus is Lord. Jesus is love. Divine power is a byproduct of love. As long as there is love, there will be power. Love mobilises power. Love utilises power. In our healing, we are healed not because God wishes to show off his power but because he demonstrates his love toward us who are sick unto death: "But God proves his love for us in that while we still were sinners Christ died for us" (Romans 5:8). The divine love of God moves any obstacle in the way to "work together for good for those who love God, who are called according to his purpose" (Romans 8:28).

Paul frames predestination as proactive love. The grace of God made a way long before Adam and Eve damaged their relationship with the Creator. God doesn't react. God the Creator is an initiator. Love initiates the outworking of power even to lay down life and take it up again for restoration to take place. God did not react to humanity's sin. God initiated reconciliation. If the loving God "did not withhold his own Son, but gave him up for all of us, will he not with him also give us everything else?" (Romans 8:32).

Paul affirms that God is for us. God is not working against love. God is for the full restoration of all things back to the originally intended purposes for relationship. God has been at work in Christ, restoring all things since the foundations of the world. Just as sin has had a grip on humankind through the fall of Adam, so it is that in Christ God had provided a way out for the generations of Adam's kind. We have a way out, and we can be safe from the self-destroying power of sin. Jesus is our Way.

QUESTIONS FOR REFLECTION OR DISCUSSION

1. What other way is there, besides the crucifixion and resurrection of Christ, to manage guilt, shame, and the effects of selfishness? Can redemption come through our own efforts?

---

2. How do you define sin?

---

3. How may we daily respond to Christ's saving grace in our salvation?

PRAYER

Lord Jesus, thank you for your obedience to the call to love us through the power of laying down your life and taking it up again so that, in you, we are saved. Thank you for your love. Thank you for your saving grace. Thank you, Lord, that you came down from heaven to earth to reveal to us the way out. Thank you for being the Way. Amen.

DAY 8

THURSDAY

WORSHIP THE LORD YOUR GOD

SCRIPTURE

MATTHEW 4:1-11

Again, the devil took him to a very high mountain and showed him
all the kingdoms of the world and their splendor; and he said to him, "All
these I will give you, if you will fall down and worship me." Jesus said to
him, "Away with you, Satan! for it is written, 'Worship the Lord
your God, and serve only him.'" Then the devil left him,
and suddenly angels came and waited on him.

—MATTHEW 4:8-11

Many are intoxicated by the idea of being worshiped. This idea—that we must be recognised and applauded for the things we do by sounding our own trumpet and drawing attention to ourselves—*ought* to be absurd in the great scheme of creation. If God is Creator, and we are created in God's image, then our own creative efforts should all point back to God, who started it all, right? Yet many of us want to keep all the credit and recognition and honor for ourselves. In today's scripture, the devil also wants to be worshiped—and, in exchange, he promises Jesus the kingdoms of the world.

The devil created nothing. The devil generates nothing but chaos. His *modus operandi* is to destroy all that the Creator has made. The devil hates anything that centres worship on God. His only intent is to destroy. Even the destruction of the environment is a way to silence worship from God's creatures. The devil is identified in Revelation as Abaddon or Apollyon, the messenger or bringer of destruction. Throughout Scripture, it is evident that he thrives on chaos. It makes sense that the one who was cut off from the source of all creation in the garden of Eden has nothing creative within himself. Cut off from the Creator, Satan is destructive. Still, this destructive force that works against love and creation seeks to be worshiped.

In 2017, a British surgeon was convicted of assault in a case where it was discovered he had branded his initials into the organs of two different patients during transplant surgeries. Humankind is desperately fallen. Some, like this surgeon, seek to stamp their importance where they have no right or privilege. There is a tendency in the fallen nature of humanity to seek glory and thanks for whatever little good we may do.

Contrast that story with the nature of the Creator, our Lord God, who quietly works behind the scenes—building, creating, inspiring, healing, nursing, feeding the birds of the air, and quietly mending bruised reeds. "All things came into being through him, and without him not one thing came into being. What has come into being in him was life, and the life was the light of all people" (John 1:3–4). Let us give him all the thanks and glory for all that he has done. Sing to the Lord in celebration with creation for his goodness that endures through all generations! Let us join in God's mission to seek and to save the lost, to restore and redeem all things. Truly the Lord is God, and only he deserves all praise and worship.

QUESTIONS FOR REFLECTION OR DISCUSSION

1. In what ways are we most like God?

_____

_____

_____

2. Why does the devil love destruction?

_____

_____

3. How do our own creative acts bear witness to God's love and grace?

_____

_____

_____

PRAYER

Lord our God, you have made the earth and all that is in it by your great love and manifest power. You heal and restore quietly, demanding nothing in return. Your love causes all things in creation to advance and prosper. We, your children, look toward the day when you will restore and redeem all things, even as creation groans in eager anticipation to fully worship you. Truly only you and you alone deserve all glory and honor and worship. Amen.

DAY 9
FRIDAY
ALL THE FAMILIES OF THE EARTH

SCRIPTURE

GENESIS 12:1–4

Now the Lord said to Abram, "Go from your country and your kindred and your father's house to the land that I will show you. I will make of you a great nation, and I will bless you, and make your name great, so that you will be a blessing. I will bless those who bless you, and the one who curses you I will curse; and in you all the families of the earth shall be blessed." So Abram went, as the Lord had told him; and Lot went with him. Abram was seventy-five years old when he departed from Haran.

—GENESIS 12:1–4

River perch—like most other fish species in KwaZulu-Natal's vast South African riverways—are hardy survivors. These fish tend to flourish in tough conditions, much like the people here. I was raised in this place just behind the Valley of a Thousand Hills. As boys, we'd duck out of church on Sunday to swim in the river and catch the perch to stock our fish tanks. The amazing thing about the fish is that, although they could live a long time in a well-maintained tank, they did not grow there. They grew old but remained miniaturised. They looked just like their large counterparts that swam in open waters, but they were dwarfed to suit their conditions.

It is amazing how our environments determine our growth. We are often limited by availability of resources, landscapes, and boundary lines, but the mission of God opens before us vistas that are unlimited in both need and opportunity, and the resources of heaven are equally unlimited. God's mission, as shared with Abraham, is that all the people of the world will be blessed. God is saying to Abraham, *"My vision is as unlimited as my love."* Abraham knows how to trust God. He knows that God's intent is to bless and progress those who trust in him. Elsewhere in Genesis we are told that Abraham "believed the Lord; and the Lord reckoned it to him as righteousness" (15:6). God promises Abraham that his presence will be sufficient for the journey.

Unlike us river boys, who selfishly took fish from open waters where they could grow and thrive, and confined them to small fish tanks, God takes Abraham from a confined world in Haran and gives him the promise of eternity. That's the power of the selfless mission. That is the power of stepping out and not knowing where we may land but trusting that God is with us (Hebrews 11:8). Someone left their comfort zone and came to my people with the gospel many years ago, trusting God in full love and obedience. Now, I am blessed and I too wish to go and be a blessing.

QUESTIONS FOR REFLECTION AND DISCUSSION

1. What are some things that confine us in reaching out to our world?

2. What are some spiritual and/or physical limitations that have prevented you from taking the gospel to others and allowing God's grace to bless "all the families of the earth"?

3. How is God leading you to be a blessing to others?

PRAYER

Lord, send us. Expand our vision beyond our comfort zones. Lord, we want to trust you and believe you like Abraham did in an act of deep, spiritual righteousness. We know that righteousness sets the standard for a loving and thriving relationship with you, God. Allow us to see the world through your love. Amen.

DAY 10
SATURDAY
MY HELP COMES FROM THE LORD

SCRIPTURE

PSALM 121

I lift up my eyes to the hills—from where will my help come?
My help comes from the Lord, who made heaven and earth. He will not
let your foot be moved; he who keeps you will not slumber. He who keeps
Israel will neither slumber nor sleep. The Lord is your keeper; the Lord is
your shade at your right hand. The sun shall not strike you by day, nor the
moon by night. The Lord will keep you from all evil; he will keep your life.
The Lord will keep your going out and your coming in from
this time on and forevermore.

—PSALM 121

An African proverb says, "When the bull elephants fight, the grass is destroyed." Blood and tears drench the soil in Africa. I cannot remember a time, growing up in South Africa, when there was a sense of prevailing peace. A state of total peace is perhaps a utopian dream anywhere, but peace and security are basic human needs. Peace comes at the grassroot level, wrapped in a fragile membrane of tolerance. Uneasy peace is probably a better description for my life experiences.

On my first visit to the United States at the turn of the century, the family hosting me in a little town in the Midwest were constantly surprised by my locking doors. I was just as surprised by their apparent comfort without the steel bars that curtain most homes in South Africa, where forces are constantly at work to mete out violence for political and economic gains. The people at the grassroots—those who are simply trying to get a piece of bread—get trampled by the elephants at war.

It is easy to imagine David's state of mind when he wrote the words of today's psalm. Anxiety, desperation, and fear ooze out of the opening line. A shepherd warrior who understands the advantage of high terrain for warfare, David says he looks to the hills. David's fighting skills were honed in the hills, where chariots and horses could not prevail. David could easily boast of his battle strategies and warfare skills, but instead he says that his help comes from the Lord.

South Africa, like many other nations, experienced high tension and civil unrest exacerbated by systemic flaws and injustices during the COVID-19 pandemic. Many neighbourhood security groups used social media to rally people to take up arms to defend their businesses, and themselves, against unrest. But our help cannot be in our sense of self-sufficiency. Our hope cannot rest in our military might. David writes that God does not sleep. God does not feel fatigued, and God does not neglect God's promises. Today's psalm affirms God's promises, provision, and protection. Truly, God moves beyond the realm of the physical threats that surround us, and arrests the powers and principalities in the heavens. Only when his will is done on earth as it is in heaven will humanity fully know the peace of God. Our help comes from the Lord.

QUESTIONS FOR REFLECTION OR DISCUSSION

1. Where, other than God, have you placed your sense of security? How has that served you?

_____

_____

_____

_____

_____

2. David was a skilled guerrilla fighter and could afford to place his trust in the rocks and elevated topography, but he chose to identify God as his source of strength. What advantage do we gain in trusting God even when we have other forms of trustworthy security available to us?

_____

_____

_____

_____

_____

PRAYER

Lord, lead us to the Rock who is higher than ourselves. We have nowhere else to turn. Where on earth could we possibly go? We have no one but you. Keep us from losing our battle against hopelessness when all we desire is you. You, O Lord, will rescue us. Amen.

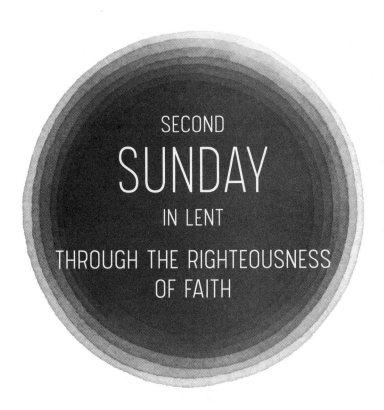

SECOND
SUNDAY
IN LENT

THROUGH THE RIGHTEOUSNESS
OF FAITH

SCRIPTURE

ROMANS 4:1–5, 13–17

For what does the scripture say? "Abraham believed God,
and it was reckoned to him as righteousness." For the promise that
he would inherit the world did not come to Abraham or to his descendants
through the law but through the righteousness of faith.

—*ROMANS 4:3, 13*

While a lot is written in these verses about Abraham, the law, the covenant, and the promise, we tend not to see what these great themes reveal about God. God in these verses is portrayed as loving, kind, relational, and true. God is revealed as trustworthy. He makes covenants based on the trust and faith Abraham displayed. God did not reward Abraham's diligence in mechanically keeping religious laws. God favoured Abraham because Abraham *believed*.

My mum's older sister was a devout Hindu. As a little boy of four or five years old, I would walk out of the house really early in the mornings and witness her ritually offer her puja (worship and prayers) to the sun using various brass vessels, water, and fire in the most ancient traditions. She concluded by marking her forehead with a reddish paste and ashes. Each day it was the same. Her consistency demonstrated her devout commitment to her faith. On the other hand, my mum became a follower of Christ. Somewhere along the line a faithful servant of God shared the good news of Jesus with my mum's family. I witnessed my mum daily offer her prayers as well. Her process was very different. It had a quality that made me believe there was actually someone in the room with us. On a number of occasions, she would walk into the room with a heavy heart and leave looking like her spirits had been completely lifted.

Mum prayed without any specific accoutrements or paraphernalia. It still gets my attention even now that her prayer and convictions are not ritualized. Mum believes God, and he reveals himself to her in ways I do not always understand. My mum has buried two sons who tragically lost their lives through trauma, leaving behind their daughters and wives. Yet I see the same uplifted look on her face each time she steps away from her prayer. Her prayer moved God's grace over me in ways I could not understand.

Rules, rites, and law only reveal their weight when such laws are violated or contravened. There can be no violation if there is no law. Some people pray obsessively in patterns of religious law just in case any change in ritual or pattern may bring calamity upon them. They take vows and carefully observe rituals and practices so tragedy does not strike. I heard a woman once say to me in church that she became sick because, the night before, she did not place her little green Bible under her pillow. Praying to appease the gods or to avoid things going wrong is a most self-centred kind of prayer. Such religious practice seeks its own ends and well-being. It is very different from the kind of prayer that seeks to love God and believe that God is faithful. Abraham believed God.

QUESTIONS FOR REFLECTION OR DISCUSSION

1. How may ritual be used to express love and devotion?

2. When does prayer become just another religious ritual, rather than a conversation with the living God?

3. How can prayer rise above mere communication with God to become communion with God?

PRAYER

Our Father in heaven, you are love. You are peace and joy. You invite us to trust you and believe in you, and on that basis, you bring us into deeper relationship with you. Lord, you fill our hearts with love and cleanse us from all selfishness. Reign on the seat of our hearts. Amen.

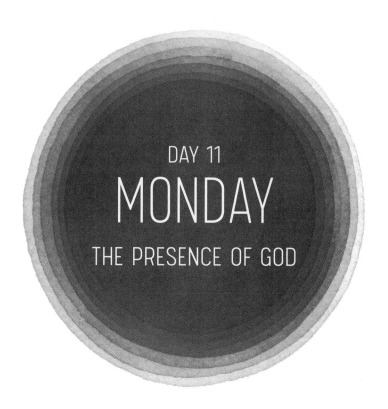

DAY 11
MONDAY
THE PRESENCE OF GOD

SCRIPTURE

JOHN 3:1–17

Now there was a Pharisee named Nicodemus, a leader of the Jews.
He came to Jesus by night and said to him, "Rabbi, we know that you
are a teacher who has come from God; for no one can do these signs
that you do apart from the presence of God." Jesus answered him,
"Very truly, I tell you, no one can see the kingdom of God
without being born from above."

—JOHN 3:1–3

There was a man who was deeply religious and always worked toward good. He defended the marginalised and spoke up for the brutalised. He was a champion, a real life hero. His name was Nicodemus. The first time we hear about him is when he approaches Jesus at night in John 3. The other two occasions we encounter him, he is helping the recently apprehended underdog, Jesus. In John 7, Nicodemus reminds his colleagues in the Sanhedrin that the law requires a person be given a hearing before being judged. In John 19, Nicodemus appears after the crucifixion to provide the customary embalming spices, and he assists Joseph of Arimathea in preparing Jesus's body for burial.

So what does Jesus see in Nicodemus that prompts him to make two of the most memorable statements in the New Testament, "You must be born again" and "For God so loved the world . . ."? Is it possible that Jesus sees a person who desperately needs relationship and not ritualised religion? In the Nicodemus references, we find a person who is ambitious, helpful, working for good, and a people pleaser. Perhaps we can add one more: Nicodemus is burning himself out looking for purpose and meaning in life.

Like in so many Middle Eastern cultures, the name given is based on the character of the individual. Nicodemus is the people's champion. That's literally what his name means in Greek: *nikos* means "hero" or "champion," and *demos* means "people." From the other gospel witnesses of his interactions with Jesus, Nicodemus is a different kind of Pharisee than his colleagues. Perhaps the thing that makes him different is that he is a defender of the people. Perhaps he genuinely sympathises with the people and, in coming to Jesus, wants to be clear in his conscience that he is indeed who he portrays himself to be. Jesus's words were faithful words. Jesus offers a strong and sincere response that seems to change the trajectory of Nicodemus's life. He comes for truth, and he receives truth in love.

Even people's champions need a champion. People's champions find it easy to burn themselves out. They need a drink of living water. People's champions need a fresh breath, and that is what Jesus offers to Nicodemus in the night. Truth. Love. Freedom. Grace. We all need life-changing encounters with sincere, honest friends who will tell us the truth about who we are and how we are perceived as leaders in the daylight hours.

QUESTIONS FOR REFLECTION OR DISCUSSION

1. How are we like Nicodemus?

2. Jesus seizes the opportunity to influence a religious leader. How important is that in our world today?

3. How do we get burned out helping others?

4. What is Jesus's advice to "the people's champion," and to us today?

PRAYER

Lord, when we are exhausted, tired, and running on empty, people still expect more from us, even when we have nothing left to give. Cleanse us with the baptism of water. Wash away our wounds and battle scars of busy, bruising days. Fill us with your Holy Spirit, that we may not be deflated in life or spirit. Work in us, Jesus. Amen.

DAY 12
TUESDAY
SUDDENLY THERE APPEARED

SCRIPTURE

MATTHEW 17:1–9

Six days later, Jesus took with him Peter and James and his brother
John and led them up a high mountain, by themselves.
And he was transfigured before them, and his face shone like the sun,
and his clothes became dazzling white. Suddenly there
appeared to them Moses and Elijah, talking with him.

—MATTHEW 17:1–3

It is comforting to know that we will know even though they did not know. My opening line is a riddle, weak as it may be. Death is the greatest of all riddles. Losing a dear loved one is one of those intensely painful experiences in life. Anybody who lives long enough will experience the death of close family members and dear friends. All of humanity will walk through the valley of death's shadow.

Personal experience has taught me the anatomy of the grieving process. There is first a deep sense of loss and a feeling of being overwhelmed. Then, almost immediately, there is denial of what has taken place. Even now, as I sit listening to updates on the violent riots taking place in my city, I have not had a chance to process the deaths of three loved ones who quietly "shuffled off the mortal coil"—to use the euphemistic line that avoids hard and real words like, "my friend died." Denial is then interrupted by guilt and/or anger for things done or not done in ways that would have produced a better quality of life. Then come the questions.

In moments of deep grief, I have questioned issues like eternity, life in Christ, and the possibility of death being a cold, grey, blank wall of permanent nothingness. I circled back to all our Middle Eastern and African religious philosophies, and while there is still meat to be picked from the bones of these philosophical explorations, one deep, prevailing question remained. *Will our loved ones know us in the afterlife?* And my opening riddle answers: It is comforting to know that we will know even though they did not know.

If Peter and the disciples collectively recognise the presence of Elijah and Moses, then I am comforted that we may recognise and know with certainty followers of Christ who have gone before us. That, however, is only a small reassurance. The real beauty of the Transfiguration text is its implication that we will know Jesus as we are known by him. While I am comforted by the possibility of knowing loved ones, and being able to hope in that is life-giving, the truly exciting piece in today's scripture is that Jesus is with those whom he has called. He will always be with us. In the words of John Wesley: "Best of all, God is with us."

QUESTIONS FOR REFLECTION OR DISCUSSION

1. What does eternal life mean to you?

_____

_____

_____

_____

_____

_____

2. In today's scripture, Elijah and Moses appear and talk with Jesus, which indicates that the spiritual realm of heaven has the ability to actively engage with earth. (See Genesis 28:12 and John 1:51 also.) What do you think? What does it mean for heaven to be that close to earth?

_____

_____

_____

_____

_____

_____

PRAYER

Lord Jesus, the life we see and experience on this side of the curtain compels us to believe that we are connected with so much more beyond this world. Open our eyes to see the realms of colours that are not visible in this world with our human eyes. Thank you for the eternal kingdom that exists unseen for now but that is making itself clearer day by day. We look to you. Thank you for watching over us. Amen.

DAY 13

WEDNESDAY

WHAT SHALL I DO WITH THIS PEOPLE?

SCRIPTURE

EXODUS 17:1–7

From the wilderness of Sin the whole congregation of the Israelites journeyed by stages, as the Lord commanded. They camped at Rephidim, but there was no water for the people to drink. The people quarreled with Moses, and said, "Give us water to drink." Moses said to them, "Why do you quarrel with me? Why do you test the Lord?" But the people thirsted there for water; and the people complained against Moses and said, "Why did you bring us out of Egypt, to kill us and our children and livestock with thirst?" So Moses cried out to the Lord, "What shall I do with this people? They are almost ready to stone me."

—*EXODUS 17:1–4*

No one can survive without water. So if people are led to a place where there is no water, it makes sense that there might be complaints. Serial complaining, however, is a very different story altogether, and that is what the Israelites have become: serial complainers. They have struggled to break themselves out of the mindset of being victims and captives. At the camp in Rephidim, the people of Israel complain yet again when they realise there is no water.

Serial complaining is a sign of a defeated life. Complaining is the language of the defeated. One of those spiritual elements that robs us of our joy is an unhealthy, unbalanced view of our self-worth in the world. Israel's people saw themselves as both victims *and* God's elect, and this tension divided their spirit. Some thought too little of themselves and therefore didn't allow God's miracles to convince them of God's faithfulness. Others thought too highly of themselves, believing they deserved so much more than the provisions God had already made for them. Manna was beneath their dignity. Their entitlement demanded meat.

As a nation, Israel went on from the wilderness to live out historic seasons of puffed-up-ness, believing they were better than most. What was meant to be their chosen distinctive of holiness essentially became their claim to exclusivity. Comparison, competition, complaining, and conflict arise from a wrong self-image. A balanced self-image comes from seeing Christlikeness in ourselves and in others. "For by the grace given to me I say to everyone among you not to think of yourself more highly than you ought to think, but to think with sober judgment, each according to the measure of faith that God has assigned" (Romans 12:3). May we walk in the power of humility. I press on to know who I am and whose I am.

QUESTIONS FOR REFLECTION OR DISCUSSION

1. How does complaining make the journey longer?

_____

_____

_____

_____

_____

_____

_____

2. What do you think of the statement "Complaining is the language of the defeated"?

_____

_____

_____

_____

_____

_____

_____

_____

PRAYER

Lord, hear our cry. Only you know our struggle. Some days, complaining and murmuring does feel good in the moment, until we discover the power of your listening ear. Prayer is our resort and resolve. Help us to remember to bring everything to you, oh Lord, in prayer.

DAY 14
THURSDAY
DO NOT HARDEN YOUR HEARTS

SCRIPTURE

PSALM 95

O come, let us sing to the Lord; let us make a joyful noise to the rock of our salvation! Let us come into his presence with thanksgiving; let us make a joyful noise to him with songs of praise! For the Lord is a great God, and a great King above all gods. Do not harden your hearts, as at Meribah, as on the day at Massah in the wilderness, when your ancestors tested me, and put me to the proof, though they had seen my work. For forty years I loathed that generation and said, "They are a people whose hearts go astray, and they do not regard my ways."

—PSALM 95:1–3, 8–10

You cannot build a strong, loving relationship on doubt and distrust. If Abraham believed God and it was counted to him as righteousness, then Israel's tribes in the wilderness confirmed that they earned the loathing of God. Verse 10 in today's psalm refers to God "loathing" a generation of Israelites for forty years—based on the way they repeatedly tested and distrusted God's faithfulness.

The God of Scripture seeks covenant. God as seen in the Old Testament may often be misunderstood as rigid, cold, and without grace, but this psalm reveals that God was deeply and profoundly loving and intent on relationship. Unlike the gods of the various cultures reflected in the Old Testament, the God of Abraham, Isaac, and Jacob was intent on being God of all nations. God is not localised or nationalised or racialised.

God promised Abraham he would be the father of all the nations of the earth. This God could not be confined to one language or identified by one ethnicity. His desire was to bring through Abraham all the people of the earth together as one people. Belief is what made Abraham a friend of God, and anyone who had faith like Abraham became a child of the faith nation.

Paul unpacks this theological truth in Romans, and it surfaces in John's writing as well. Jesus's action of cleansing the temple and his utterance that God's house will be a house of prayer for all nations, which is a direct reference to Isaiah, reiterates God's desire for covenant and relationship across diverse demographic and identity lines. Quality relationships have a deep essential belief in partnership. Trust and love are built first on the act of believing.

QUESTIONS FOR REFLECTION OR DISCUSSION

1. What is the foundation of your relationship with God?

_____

_____

_____

_____

2. How have you experienced quality of life when distrust is prevalent in a relationship?

_____

_____

_____

_____

3. What does it mean to you to have received the right of adoption as a child of God?

_____

_____

_____

_____

_____

PRAYER

Dear Lord Jesus, we thank you for your grace that inspires our hearts to believe. You sought us out, and we believe in you. You love us and have justified us, and your love draws our hearts to repentance. You invested your life for us long before we knew we were worth loving. You are the rock that quenches our thirst, and we love you. Amen.

DAY 15
FRIDAY
POURED INTO OUR HEARTS

SCRIPTURE

ROMANS 5:1–11

Therefore, since we are justified by faith, we have peace with God through our Lord Jesus Christ, through whom we have obtained access to this grace in which we stand; and we boast in our hope of sharing the glory of God. And not only that, but we also boast in our sufferings, knowing that suffering produces endurance, and endurance produces character, and character produces hope, and hope does not disappoint us, because God's love has been poured into our hearts through the Holy Spirit that has been given to us.

—ROMANS 5:1–5

"Suffering" and "glory" are two words that don't seem to fit in the same space at face value. The longer I ponder on the subject, however, the more these concepts draw closer to each other. Fire walkers and ultra-marathon runners, for example, understand suffering paired with glory. There's something long-term about the development of strength and stamina in the suffering that lends itself to the reward of the glory.

The layering concept of suffering that produces endurance and endurance that produces character and character that produces hope, is amazing. The imagery that comes to mind is that of an oyster laboring to produce a pearl. Deep in the sea, the oyster picks up an agitant, a mere speck of debris—an unnatural condition in the life cycle of the oyster. The oyster tries to rid itself of the irritant by secreting a serum that engulfs the speck. Over time the irritant becomes trapped in the smooth layers of nacre that form the pearl. The layers of nacre are like the layers that shape our character and, ultimately, our hope. Hope shines forth after having endured the pain of sin, that unnatural irritant, which only grace could contain, and which gives rise to something different in and through our lives. Christ in us takes our sin, becoming formed in us, his glory reigning in us.

The order of suffering and glory follows the order of cross before crown. In our endurance, our faith is strengthened, and in a strong faith, character is evident. Christ in us, that hope of glory, is manifest in the strength of our character. Faith that holds on and does not quickly deny our convictions emerges as glorious hope that never disappoints. This is the process by which God makes all things beautiful.

There were days in my life when the weight of glory developing in my spirit felt like too much to bear. I was tempted at times to abandon the cause and free myself from the heaviness of the pearl forming within. When you find yourself being tempted in that same way, hold on! Something glorious is taking place. The flesh within the oyster is displaced by the growing pearl. The more the glorious pearl grows, the more the flesh diminishes, and soon "we have peace with God through our Lord Jesus Christ." Ultimately, Christ is formed in us, and we are saved for his glorious purpose.

QUESTIONS FOR REFLECTION OR DISCUSSION

1. How is Christ being formed in you?

2. How do you see spiritual formation taking place in your life right now?

3. How is Christ in you emerging as the hope of glory?

PRAYER

Lord, keep us strong when it feels like the weight of hope and glory forming within us is too much to bear. We hold on in the hope of what is to come in the shaping process of suffering, which produces endurance and ultimately the formation of Christ in us. May your glory shine through us.
Amen.

DAY 16
SATURDAY
GOD PROVES HIS LOVE FOR US

SCRIPTURE

ROMANS 5:1-11

For while we were still weak, at the right time Christ died for the ungodly.
Indeed, rarely will anyone die for a righteous person—
though perhaps for a good person someone might actually
dare to die. But God proves his love for us in that while
we still were sinners Christ died for us.

—ROMANS 5:6-8

The story has been told so often, but it still has strong value. The little girl jumped up and down in the seat as the jet made its way to the airport where she was to meet her dad. She unbuckled herself and ran around excitedly like a Ms. Pac-Man in a dress. She feasted on the doughnuts and Coke and the other snacks. More doughnuts, more soda, and the layering and the jumping by the miniature Ms. Pac-Man continued for an hour. Then the pilot came on the intercom and delivered the obligatory message: "Ladies and gentlemen, we are going to make our descent shortly, and there will be mild turbulence." Anyone who flies frequently will tell you that such a message is code for "hold onto your stomachs and pray."

The story goes that the doughnut-eating, soda-guzzling little girl experienced the full might of the turbulence. After the eruption, she was covered in her own vomit. Mum tried hurriedly to wipe her down and make her presentable. But it was time to leave the plane. They made their way to the arrivals lounge, and no sooner did they arrive than in walked Daddy. He was beaming with smiles, excited to see his baby after missing her for many days. He ran toward his family and, without hesitating, picked up his little girl in all her sogginess and with bits of undigested cake still clinging to her clothes. He pressed her close, without a care for his nice suit, and loved her.

"But God proves his love for us in that while we still were sinners Christ died for us." We are loved, and God does is not deterred from loving us by the filth of the world that stains us. He sees the image of himself within us. That is where the true value lies. The sin and sinful ways of the world cannot denature us. We are God's, and God is ours. God is our Father, our *Abba*, who loves us and holds us to himself without hesitation. In him we find our place and our belonging.

QUESTIONS FOR REFLECTION OR DISCUSSION

1. God does not expect for us to first cleanse ourselves then come to him. He draws us to himself then cleanses us. How does this affirm your salvation experience?

_____

_____

_____

_____

2. How can we work toward helping ourselves and others understand that God does not expect us to cleanse ourselves before coming to stand in his presence and grace?

_____

_____

_____

_____

3. What do you understand by the statement "While we still were sinners Christ died for us"?

_____

_____

_____

_____

PRAYER

Lord Jesus, you gave yourself for us even before the foundations of the world were laid. You loved us, and when we heard of your love for us, we could not remain passive. We thank you for your love and your grace. Your love draws us to repentance. Amen.

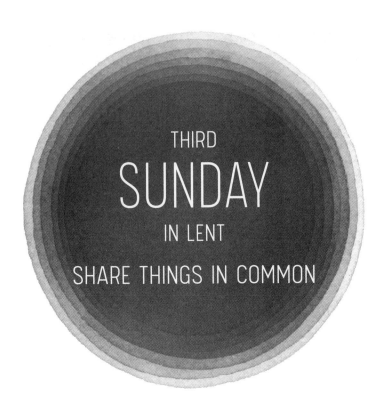

THIRD
SUNDAY
IN LENT

SHARE THINGS IN COMMON

SCRIPTURE

JOHN 4:1–42

So he came to a Samaritan city called Sychar, near the plot of ground that Jacob had given to his son Joseph. Jacob's well was there, and Jesus, tired out by his journey, was sitting by the well. It was about noon. A Samaritan woman came to draw water, and Jesus said to her, "Give me a drink." (His disciples had gone to the city to buy food.) The Samaritan woman said to him, "How is it that you, a Jew, ask a drink of me, a woman of Samaria?" (Jews do not share things in common with Samaritans.)

—JOHN 4:5–9

Anyone who has served the church for more than a few months will soon learn that tough conversations are inevitable. We must engage in love and decide to love in spite of tough conversations and conclusions. I was raised in a system known for keeping ethnic groups apart. "Separated," "unequal," "brutal," "dehumanizing," "suspicious," and "contemptuous" are words that come to mind as byproducts of that system. To have a person of a different skin colour in one's home was illegal at the height of apartheid in South Africa. The different ethnic and race groups were relegated to specific geographical areas. People of colour risked life and limb if caught in a forbidden community without the necessary work permits. Some groups were given the right-of-way: walking on the sidewalk was for the privileged, and a person of colour was supposed to step onto the road if a person of racial privilege walked on the sidewalk.

Jesus was privileged. If that statement seems off to you, allow me to explain. Given his context, Jesus is perceived as the privileged one when compared to the woman at the well. Jesus is male and Jewish. She is a woman, a Samaritan, and is excluded even by her own people. At the well in Samaria, race, gender, and privilege meet. The well reveals our human need to live—to have basic needs met like thirst, hunger, rest, and recreation. When Jesus asks the woman for a drink she may be assuming that he expects the people of Samaria to meet his needs because many Jews see themselves as "better" than Samaritans. Afterall, he has brought nothing to the well, but he still expects to be given a drink. Racism and prejudice raise unwarranted suspicion. That is the hurt of racism, and it does damage to both sides. Preconceived ideas born in the fires of hate feed the worldview of those trapped in ironic prejudice.

An example of ironic prejudice is the disciples of Jesus in this scene, and their quest for food. An all-Jewish band of hungry men who have social dominance over Samaritans descend upon a village of Samaritans to buy food. They purchase from the very people group the average Jew despises. The irony speaks volumes: "We are better, and they are not good enough in every other way, but we will trust them to take care of one of our most basic needs." A similar scenario played out in South Africa when many of the oppressed people of colour were employed to cook, clean, and raise the children of the privileged few—and of course many social structures built on oppression have seen this pattern play out in their contexts. It may be ironic, even hypocritical, but it does not change the fact that it is prejudice. How does Jesus treat the issue?

Jesus sees the worth of the woman. Her intrinsic worth is the purpose of his redemptive mission. The disciples see the Samaritans as valuable only in terms of their labour. Jesus completely restructures the social hierarchy of the village. By the time he is done affirming the woman's personal worth, people are asking him (the Jewish man) to stay, and looking beyond social classification as they recognise Jesus to be the Saviour of the world.

The world needs that Jesus perspective on worth right now. The world needs people to be restored in their self-worth and personal value, seeing themselves in the image of God and beginning to imitate the ways of God in the world. Kindness, justice, and humility flow out of the heart of God and are the bedrock of all successful societies. That's what Jesus demonstrates to the woman at the well, and it flows into the community as healing.

QUESTIONS FOR REFLECTION OR DISCUSSION

1. How are we blinded from seeing the image of God in others?

_____

_____

_____

_____

2. How can we be instrumental in freeing the image of God in others?

_____

_____

_____

_____

3. What implicit prejudicial messages exist in the way we treat those of different race, social status, or even church denomination?

_____

_____

_____

_____

PRAYER

God of love and peace, help us to see you in every image-bearer whom you have created. Allow us to celebrate your hand of creative varieties in all. May we grow wise and complete in celebrating diversity. Help us to celebrate differences and not be divisive. Grant that we may be peacemakers and restorers of your image in the most broken among us.
Amen.

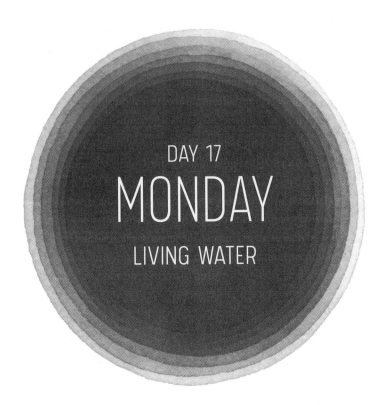

DAY 17

MONDAY

LIVING WATER

SCRIPTURE

JOHN 4:1–42

Jesus answered her, "If you knew the gift of God, and who it is that is saying to you, 'Give me a drink,' you would have asked him, and he would have given you living water." The woman said to him, "Sir, you have no bucket, and the well is deep. Where do you get that living water? Are you greater than our ancestor Jacob, who gave us the well, and with his sons and his flocks drank from it?" Jesus said to her, "Everyone who drinks of this water will be thirsty again, but those who drink of the water that I will give them will never be thirsty. The water that I will give will become in them a spring of water gushing up to eternal life." The woman said to him, "Sir, give me this water, so that I may never be thirsty or have to keep coming here to draw water."

—JOHN 4:10–15

Some hold the view that the woman at the well represents humanity in need of physical restoration, replenishment, and refreshing. The conversation with Jesus begins with the need for water and food but quickly leads to a political conversation when she points out his Jewish identity and then becomes a religious conversation when Jesus brings up God. The text reveals three basic human needs: physical refreshment and rest, a clear bearing on reality, and solid, authentic relationships.

First, we all need *refreshing*. By that I mean physical rest. The automation of our society has led to newer technology that demands higher speeds. Every day we are bombarded with a need for faster, better, more. We crave sugar and caffeine to help us cope with the speed of life. Have we lost the vitality of our lives? One of our greatest needs is physical restoration. It's no different from this moment in the life of the Samaritan woman. Even Jesus at the well needs food, water, and rest.

Second, we all need a serious dose of *reality*. The entertainment industry reveals a great need for reality-based entertainment. Youth are no longer hungry for pipe dreams and political spin doctors. The desperate search for reality forces many to buy into the different dreams of rehashed ideologies of ancient religions. People are hungry for truth because people are starved for a better reality. Some think wealth is the only reality. They believe it is the only way to live. Yet money and the absence of money can give us a reality check we may not want. Some really miserable people have unlimited access to money. Others say health is the answer. If you've got health, you've got everything. That is really more of a faith statement. After all, who can guarantee good health in a high-speed world? Still others believe education is the way, the truth, and the life. Others promote spiritualism, nudism, yoga, meditation—you name it, someone has it and calls it reality. This is the thirsty life. Ask the woman at the well. The person who seeks what is real will find it only in the holy, loving God. The person who wants to live out their purpose on earth will only find meaning in the Creator. In trying to understand the purpose and design of a machine, we never ask the *machine* to reveal its purpose. The manufacturer knows the function of the machine before it even comes into existence and installs within it the form for its function.

Third, we need authentic, dependable *relationships*. A right relationship with God brings us into alignment with community and faith. This doesn't mean that, if you love God, everyone will love you. Most in Jesus's world do not fully understand him, and many reject him. It will very likely be the same for those who follow Jesus. But those who are of the household of faith will see the Spirit of Christ in us and will welcome us.

At the well, Jesus demonstrates the woman's deep desire for meaningful relationships by revealing to her that her external situations are telling of her internal condition. God uses external situations to reveal to us our internal condition. How can we possibly attain this life of balanced rest, reality, and relationships? The apostle John argues that it is in the water we drink, by which he means the Holy Spirit. Whoever thirsts will be filled with the Spirit and will thirst no more (see John 7: 37–39). May the Spirit bring balance and fulfilment to the basic needs of our lives.

QUESTIONS FOR REFLECTION OR DISCUSSION

1. What is your greatest need right now? Rest? A dose of reality through the eyes of Jesus? Relationships that add value and health?

2. What can you do to actively seek and be given what you need from Jesus?

3. What external situations are currently revealing to you your internal condition?

PRAYER

Lord, complete your work in us. Cleanse our hearts from all that draws us away from our inner peace and your design. Restore unto us joy through rest, reality, and relationships in you. Amen.

DAY 18
TUESDAY
I WILL SHOW YOU WHAT YOU SHALL DO

SCRIPTURE

1 SAMUEL 16:1–13

The Lord said to Samuel, "How long will you grieve over Saul? I have rejected him from being king over Israel. Fill your horn with oil and set out; I will send you to Jesse the Bethlehemite, for I have provided for myself a king among his sons." Samuel said, "How can I go? If Saul hears of it, he will kill me." And the Lord said, "Take a heifer with you, and say, 'I have come to sacrifice to the Lord.' Invite Jesse to the sacrifice, and I will show you what you shall do; and you shall anoint for me the one whom I name to you." Samuel did what the Lord commanded, and came to Bethlehem. The elders of the city came to meet him trembling, and said, "Do you come peaceably?" He said, "Peaceably; I have come to sacrifice to the Lord; sanctify yourselves and come with me to the sacrifice." And he sanctified Jesse and his sons and invited them to the sacrifice.

—1 SAMUEL 16:1–5

Does God have conversations with us the way Samuel enjoyed conversations with God? Today's scripture contains a wonderful story concerning the selection of the successor to King Saul. What strikes me is that the story develops within a conversation the prophet Samuel has with God. Samuel first heard God call him when he was young (see 1 Samuel 3), and he has never forgotten God's voice. All throughout Scripture, it is evident that God speaks frankly and openly with God's people: Job, Elijah, Moses, Hannah, and the list goes on. Some have epiphanies, others have theophanies, and still more have dreams and visions. Whatever the method, God speaks to God's people. Does he still?

God does not merely speak to people in the Bible; God seems to *interact* and go back and forth with people. In today's scripture, God strategizes with Samuel. Samuel is afraid that if he enters this town with the notice that he is auditioning potential new kings, then Saul will lose his cool and Samuel will lose his head. So he puts that concern out before God, and God offers up a plan in return. Wow! I need that kind of conversation. Can you imagine having God as your advisor in the board room? Or imagine having God as our chief counsel in the government. What would that look like?

I think God advises and offers counsel all the time. I believe God is saying even today: "I want to see my will done on earth as it is in heaven." The reality, though, is that while God strategizes and motivates in counsel, God still requires a person who is listening and willing to act on God's behalf. There is something necessary and important about being tuned in to God's frequency. God is always making known his desires for us. Are we tuned in to the frequency and wavelength of the Spirit of the Lord?

It was a Jesus Film Project night. The Jesus Film was an evangelism outreach tool that we as a local church used to present the gospel. It was my birthday in 2001. My parents took me out to dinner. After dinner I knew the team was out on the field. I wanted to go home and wind down with my family, but I had a sense of restlessness, a need to go check on the team.

When I arrived, everything looked normal. It was Friday, and there was a good crowd. I greeted the team leader and turned to leave when I sensed the curious nudge again. Then I noticed a young woman seated on a chair in a darkened corner. Everyone else in the crowd was standing.

I walked up to the woman and introduced myself and Mary, my wife. We chatted with her a little, and I asked her why she was seated. She explained that she could not walk.

At that moment, I was filled with confidence and a prompting from God in my heart, saying, *"Pray with her."*

In a few moments, the woman was walking in front of all her neighbours. Jesus showed up in that moment. God was there. Many were saved by the love and grace of Jesus that night.

Tuned in, obedient, and sensitive to the ways of God—that's how I see Samuel in today's text. There is a deep element of absolute trust, total commitment, and eager willingness to do what God asks of us that brings a manifestation of his love in powerful ways.

QUESTIONS FOR REFLECTION OR DISCUSSION

1. What can we do to better tune in to God's communication frequency?

   _____

   _____

   _____

   _____

2. How do the many social distractions and voices from crowds block our communication with God?

   _____

   _____

   _____

   _____

3. What is the value of spiritual obedience?

   _____

   _____

   _____

   _____

   _____

PRAYER

Lord, help us to be sensitive to your voice. Teach us to familiarize ourselves with your voice and know your heart's desire. Lord, we desire to be like Samuel, who first heard your call and then never forgot your voice. We are here, Lord. Hear our hearts. Speak to us. Commune with us. Amen.

DAY 19
WEDNESDAY
THIS IS THE ONE

SCRIPTURE

1 SAMUEL 16:1–13

Jesse made seven of his sons pass before Samuel, and Samuel said to Jesse, "The Lord has not chosen any of these." Samuel said to Jesse, "Are all your sons here?" And he said, "There remains yet the youngest, but he is keeping the sheep." And Samuel said to Jesse, "Send and bring him; for we will not sit down until he comes here." He sent and brought him in. Now he was ruddy, and had beautiful eyes, and was handsome. The Lord said, "Rise and anoint him; for this is the one." Then Samuel took the horn of oil, and anointed him in the presence of his brothers; and the spirit of the Lord came mightily upon David from that day forward. Samuel then set out and went to Ramah.

—1 SAMUEL 16:10–13

I am sure today's scripture is often preached in messages about judging a book by its cover. We have all heard the narrative about how it was the unassuming, smelly shepherd boy who was chosen to be king—and we're going to hear about it again! As Samuel goes down the line of David's brothers, he is ready to bestow the anointing oil upon anyone who looks princely and stately. Samuel looks at the outward appearance. He considers height, appearance, and all the other qualities most people look for in an influencer. But those are not what God looks at.

Smelly, youthful, and left out in the cold may be better descriptors for young David. He is certainly not the fancy bottle of perfume set under special lights in the high-end store. As I read this passage, I think about how little the world has changed since David's anointing. People still seek out the fancy, impressive packaging. Marketing psychology talks about branding and recognition, all the while encouraging brands to bait the customer by appealing to the senses. I cannot begin to calculate my buyer's remorse due to the gullibility I have had for fishing equipment. In the department of fancy, flashy things, fishing equipment is often designed to catch the fishers more so than the fish.

God looks at the substance within. It is not a secret that God truly looks at our personal, intrinsic worth and not our external, worldly worth. The story of the seven-year-old girl with the fancifully wrapped gift brings this truth to light. It was the week before school let out for the Christmas season. Siphiwe went to school and delicately brought out of her bag a beautiful, crisp, pearly white, precisely wrapped cube, adorned with shiny gold bows, bells, and curly red ribbons. To the awe of her classmates, the little box sat unopened on her desk, garnering fanciful guesses and wonder about what could be inside. By day two, kids were peeping through the doors, passing by staring, and wondering out loud. It proved too much for inquisitive Khanye, Siphiwe's best friend. She got in early one morning, minutes before anyone else arrived, and ripped open the package. Bows, bells, and ribbons lay strewn on the floor next to the chunk of empty cardboard and pearly white paper. That was all there was to it. Fancy on the outside. Empty of anything meaningful on the inside.

God loves the weight of worth within us. God sees the image we bear first from within. It is easier to fix up the outside and fit it for service than it is to bring forth the worth and wealth of character from within. That is exactly what the Creator wants to do. God builds worth from within. Like the baby in the manger wrapped in discarded old cloths, the stable and the manger are given eternal value not because of anything rich and fanciful on the outside but because of the great gift that lay within. That same Christ can and is transforming our lives from the inside out. He adds value, giving our lives greater worth than all the wealth in the world.

QUESTIONS FOR REFLECTION OR DISCUSSION

1. How do you measure your worth in this world?

_____

_____

_____

_____

_____

_____

_____

2. How do you measure your worth and value to the community around you?

_____

_____

_____

_____

_____

_____

_____

PRAYER

Lord create in us pure hearts. Let the weight of your beauty be seen in and through us. Lord, we do not wish to be whitewashed tombs on the outside filled with dead bones on the inside. Lord, as the old hymn says, "let the beauty of Jesus be seen in us." Amen.

DAY 20
THURSDAY
THE LORD IS MY SHEPHERD

SCRIPTURE

PSALM 23

The LORD is my shepherd, I shall not want. He makes me lie down in green pastures; he leads me beside still waters; he restores my soul. He leads me in right paths for his name's sake. Even though I walk through the darkest valley, I fear no evil; for you are with me; your rod and your staff—they comfort me. You prepare a table before me in the presence of my enemies; you anoint my head with oil; my cup overflows. Surely goodness and mercy shall follow me all the days of my life, and I shall dwell in the house of the LORD my whole life long.

—PSALM 23

Psalm 23 speaks about the work of God in our lives. There is a mutual understanding in the relationship between shepherd and flock. I have no problem accepting that God has his place and I have mine. In this psalm I understand that I have my place in light of the shepherd's place. I like my place. I love God's presence. My place is to trust. My place is to follow and learn. The more I grow in trust and knowledge, the more the gap between the way I am and the way God sees me diminishes. Under the Shepherd's care, I become more the way he desires me to be.

When I trust him, I give way to his desires for my life. "Many plans are in a person's heart, but the advice of the LORD will stand" (Proverbs 19:21, NASB). When I allow God to lead, my desires for my life also become clear and desirable. There's rest, refreshment, and relationship in God's presence when I simply trust him. That's the point of spiritual formation. My entire objective as a follower of the Shepherd is to love and trust until all fear is displaced. I love and trust until self-reliance is gone. The ancient shepherd spent days identifying places to rest the sheep. He worked tirelessly to bring health and healing to the flock that depended on him. That is why the psalmist could write with great confidence, "The Lord is my shepherd, I shall not want." Even death cannot intimidate the timid sheep because of the shepherd's presence.

If the shepherd's presence is life and light, the absence of the shepherd means that shadows grow larger when the light gets dimmer. Hence, I will always seek to walk in his light. Small things cast great shadows in the wrong light. Hence, I will always seek to walk in the light of him in whom there are no shifting shadows. Shadows cannot physically harm me. The light reveals that shadows have no substance. There is nothing in a shadow that can be trusted as real, so I will not focus my attention on shadows. Don't focus on the shadows around you. Focus on the Shepherd ahead of you. He is able to do exceedingly more than we can think of or ask for.

QUESTIONS FOR REFLECTION OR DISCUSSION

1. What does it mean to be a sheep in the presence of a shepherd?

2. How can obedience be a form of worship?

3. What does it mean to you to know the difference between the work of the shepherd and the place of the sheep?

PRAYER

Lord, you are the Good Shepherd. No one in the world leads like you. Your heart is for your flock. You desire the very best for those who desire to dwell in your presence forever. Today we affirm that we desire to be in no other place except in your presence, always. Amen.

DAY 21

FRIDAY

CHILDREN OF LIGHT

SCRIPTURE

EPHESIANS 5:8–14

For once you were darkness, but now in the Lord you are light. Live as children of light—for the fruit of the light is found in all that is good and right and true. Try to find out what is pleasing to the Lord. Take no part in the unfruitful works of darkness, but instead expose them. For it is shameful even to mention what such people do secretly; but everything exposed by the light becomes visible, for everything that becomes visible is light. Therefore it says, "Sleeper, awake! Rise from the dead, and Christ will shine on you."

—*EPHESIANS 5:8–14*

Light is a form of energy. The sun is a glorious example that light energy is transferable and indestructible. That which cannot radiate light suffers the absence of it. Light, in a very basic form, is also a source of warmth. Darkness and cold are the manifest absence of light and warmth.

In Ephesians, the apostle Paul takes time to unpack the theology of the headship of Christ. The letter to the Ephesians gives a clear understanding of the foundational power of Christ and his work in the adoption of those who "once were far off" (2:13). Paul then describes how those who were brought near ought to dwell in unity as the church of Jesus. In Ephesians, Paul presents Jesus as the light shining through the church.

Jesus is the ultimate purpose and cause for love and light. He is also the way the light of reason and the light of love are reintroduced to a darkened world. Paul explains that the audience—and, by application, we—were once darkness, devoid of the light of Christ. Now we are light. It is wonderful to know that, although we may not be the source of light, we may be like the moon, reflecting the light. The moon remains in proximity and relationship with the sun and becomes vital to the seasons of the earth.

Jesus said, "Let your light shine before others, so that they may see your good works and give glory to your Father in heaven" (Matthew 5:16). The world could do with great light and clarity to walk in love.

QUESTIONS FOR REFLECTION OR DISCUSSION

1. Why is it important to radiate the light of Christ?

_____

_____

_____

_____

_____

_____

2. How are you reflecting the light? Does your reflection also bring warmth?

_____

_____

_____

_____

_____

_____

_____

PRAYER

Lord, let your light shine brightly through us. Shine in us and through us so that others may see you and know your way. We are lost without your light in our lives. Bring forth fruit from the light we carry. Dispel the fruitless works of darkness. May we be warmth, light, and hope in the darkened world. Amen.

DAY 22
SATURDAY
LIGHT OF THE WORLD

SCRIPTURE

JOHN 9:1-41

"As long as I am in the world, I am the light of the world."
When he had said this, he spat on the ground and made mud with
the saliva and spread the mud on the man's eyes, saying to him,
"Go, wash in the pool of Siloam" (which means Sent). Then he
went and washed and came back able to see.

—*JOHN 9:5-7*

In yesterday's Ephesians scripture, we read from Paul that "everything exposed by the light becomes visible" (5:13). The text opens our eyes to see the wonder-working power of love through the Light of the world. Jesus reveals that what seems like a state of permanent brokenness to humanity is a great challenge to the God of all creation. While we explore today's text on blindness, may our eyes also be opened to the marvellous depth of vision God is able to restore. In this passage, not only is the blind man able to see, but the audience hearing and reading the story can also have a revelation of spiritual sight.

What happens in today's text? What light does Jesus shed on himself by opening the blind man's eyes? Does Jesus need to physically touch or use matter in order to perform a miracle? As the Gospels reveal, the centurion's servant is healed from a distance (Matthew 8:5–13), and Lazarus is raised to life from the spoken word from outside the tomb (John 11:1–44). On the other hand, Jesus also turns water into wine (John 2:1–12) and multiplies bread and fish to feed thousands of people (Matthew 14:13–21; 15:32–39; Mark 6:30–44; 8:1–10; Luke 9:10–17; John 6:1–15). In today's story, Jesus spits on the soil and makes mud for the man's eyes. What is this about? I have always maintained that, in all of these examples, Jesus is demonstrating that he is truly God.

Jesus seals the revelation of who he really was by using the elements of the earth. Jesus demonstrates that time and matter are subject to him. Jesus is the author of the laws of nature and science. He is God— who exists far above time and matter. By turning water into wine, the Lord demonstrates that time can be compressed. Harvest time and production time—in fact, all time, belongs and is subject to him. He compresses time and short-circuits the very systems he has set in place in our universe. He stretched time and contracts it again by making mud for the man's eyes. Every technology and gadget for centuries to come lies trapped within that ball of mud. Jesus masterfully unlocks it all to effect healing in the man's eyes. Like plasticity and clay, it all comes together in the master's hand, and the earth brings forth all things in response to God's love for his people.

Jesus does not demonstrate his power in these examples. He demonstrates his love, which unlocks the power to bring provision, protection, and promise to life. And it is the same today. His love unlocks the elements and environment around us to bring forth his healing grace.

QUESTIONS FOR REFLECTION OR DISCUSSION

1. How have you experienced God's power motivated by his love?

    _____

    _____

    _____

    _____

    _____

    _____

2. How are the environments around you able to respond to Christ's call to love?

    _____

    _____

    _____

    _____

    _____

    _____

PRAYER

Lord Jesus, thank you for your love that is manifested in your authority and power over the elements around us. You are Lord of all, and your love is manifest through all things subject to you. Thank you for bringing light to every darkened corner of our fallen world. Amen.

FOURTH
SUNDAY
IN LENT

AND THEY WERE DIVIDED

SCRIPTURE

JOHN 9:1-41

Then the Pharisees also began to ask him how he had received his sight. He said to them, "He put mud on my eyes. Then I washed, and now I see." Some of the Pharisees said, "This man is not from God, for he does not observe the sabbath." But others said, "How can a man who is a sinner perform such signs?" And they were divided. So they said again to the blind man, "What do you say about him? It was your eyes he opened." He said, "He is a prophet."

—JOHN 9:15-17

Many times, like the Pharisees, I have added confusion to those who were sincerely seeking truth in Christ. We Christians are divided in our opinions about basic theological interpretations, and sadly, we often place those stumbling blocks of confusion in front of crowds. When we present ourselves to the world as people who claim to know God yet are divided among ourselves about the actions and dealings of God in the world, we add to the blindness and confusion of those who are most needy among us.

I have a host of friends on my social media networks. Many of my friends are actual friends and acquaintances whom I know and have met in person. Many are not Christ followers. Therefore, I do not debate religion and theology on my social media platforms because I refuse to add confusion to anyone's search for life and meaning in Christ. I do welcome questions, reasoning together, and conversation.

The religious leaders in today's text add confusion to the situation. What should be a huge celebration of the restoration of sight in the man's life becomes blindness to the facts and a prevailing ignorance of the law for everyone. Law and love are not contradictory in the gospel of Jesus. All the laws were given by God as a measure of protection and as an expression of love for God's people. Laws reveal the boundary lines within which relationships of trust and dependence function. The law protects relationships. To exalt the law to the detriment of love is to miss the point of the law. Sabbath is not a law to follow for its own sake. Sabbath is a law to protect and offer rest for the weary. Sabbath heals. Therefore, there is no contradiction in practice. Sabbath, as well as the act of restoring the man's sight, are both about healing. Love is the point.

Laws in and of themselves fail all the time, but love never fails. When we completely understand that keeping the law is truly about others and maintaining safe boundaries for others to flourish, then the law is effective as an expression of love. "Let love be genuine; hate what is evil, hold fast to what is good; love one another with mutual affection; outdo one another in showing honor" (Romans 12:9–10). May God help us work to find the truth and principle of the law as an expression of his love. The practice of healing on the Sabbath is the ultimate act of giving rest to the hurting and broken child of God. It is the ultimate fulfilment of the law of love.

QUESTIONS FOR REFLECTION OR DISCUSSION

1. How should Christ followers engage each other and nonbelievers on social media? How can our public conversations and disagreements offer salvation and healing for the lost?

2. How may we add value to those seeking a way in Christ?

3. How do you use social media? To communicate hope and draw people toward Christ? To divide and confuse? To stay silent?

PRAYER

Lord Jesus, help us use every public platform we have to communicate truth and authenticity from lives that have been transformed by your love and grace. Help us to celebrate your work and grace publicly as we bear witness to your presence through your Holy Spirit. May we add clarity and not confusion concerning your love and laws. Amen.

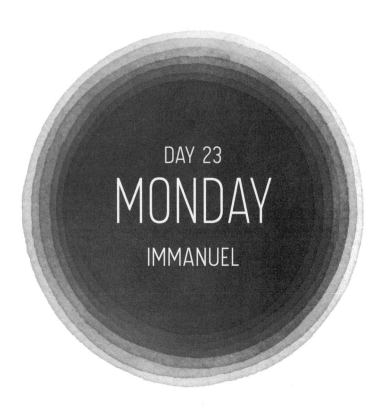

DAY 23
MONDAY
IMMANUEL

SCRIPTURE

ISAIAH 7:10–14

Again the LORD spoke to Ahaz, saying, Ask a sign of the LORD your God;
let it be deep as Sheol or high as heaven. But Ahaz said, I will not ask,
and I will not put the LORD to the test. Then Isaiah said: "Hear then,
O house of David! Is it too little for you to weary mortals, that you
weary my God also? Therefore the Lord himself will give you a sign.
Look, the young woman is with child and shall bear a son,
and shall name him Immanuel."

—ISAIAH 7:10–14

Matthew echoes today's scripture in his Gospel: "She will give birth to a son, and you are to give him the name Jesus, because he will save his people from their sins" (Matthew 1:21, NIV). The best of heaven was given for the worst on earth. He came as our hope and peace. "All this took place to fulfill what the Lord had said through the prophet: 'The virgin will conceive and give birth to a son, and they will call him Immanuel' (which means 'God with us')" (1:22–23, NIV). The name Jesus means "the Lord saves." Immanuel means "God with us." No matter what we face, God is with us and will save us from destructive thoughts, choices, and destructive systems. Somehow the presence of Christ invites me to commit my way to him, and he will direct my path as the one who is with me.

A story is told of a group of tribal youth who accompanied an early missionary into the northern parts of KwaZulu-Natal. Exhausted from the gruelling journey, the missionary fell to the ground and lay gasping for air. The young men closest to him fell down beside him and began to blow long breaths of air on the missionary's face and neck until he cooled down. In his preaching the missionary later went on to talk about that moment of desperate helplessness when he experienced the full understanding of Immanuel. He stated that he understood in practice what it meant to have the one who is close to us fall down beside us to raise us back up. The one who is with us is he who blows his breath of life upon us.

That seems to be the solid bedrock of faith. God is with us on the journey. God is resuscitating us on the journey. Whether you are walking through a deep, dark valley or lying alone in a hospital bed, God is with you. Some may be going through a crisis of relationship. God is with you. Perhaps you are carrying guilt for a habit you cannot break. Here's the good news. God is not just *with* you. God is *for* you. He desires to speak release of life and freedom to us. Jesus desires to set you free.

The miracle of a virgin who gave birth to a baby still overwhelms my thinking. If God can undertake the impossible in the virgin birth, then the idea of the Holy Spirit coming to dwell in my life—displacing my urge to self-govern—is very real. The idea of God living in me in the power of the Spirit, filling me with love that casts out all fear, is very reasonable and most appealing. In the first part of the prophetic writings of Isaiah, the text reveals that it is not for us to test God. It is for us to trust God in the signs God has given to us to reassure us. God has essentially placed us in the care of the one who is with us when we fail, fatigued and fallen to the ground. Jesus is our resuscitator. Immanuel—God with us.

QUESTIONS FOR REFLECTION OR DISCUSSION

1. When have you experienced the life-giving closeness of Jesus?

2. When has Immanuel showed up and turned a situation around for you?

3. How did you respond to the close presence of the one who resuscitates us?

PRAYER

Lord, our God, the one who stays close to us. Thank you for breathing life upon us in moments when we are at our weakest. Your presence is truly heaven. Abide with us. We invite you to stay not just beside us but to come and dwell within us. Amen.

DAY 24
TUESDAY
SCEPTER OF EQUITY

SCRIPTURE

PSALM 45

Your throne, O God, endures forever and ever. Your royal scepter
is a scepter of equity; you love righteousness and hate wickedness.
Therefore God, your God, has anointed you with the oil
of gladness beyond your companions.

—PSALM 45:6–7

I have served as a pastor for more than twenty years. After many years of meeting couples at the altar, weddings have become one of my many favourite occasions. I particularly like Eastern-themed weddings. The colours, the dancing, the aromatic and perfumed drapery all around the hall, and the sumptuous feasts for queens and kings cannot be ignored. There are long poems and fancy dances around the high chairs (or thrones). Gift exchanges build bonds between the families. The older ones nudge the younger into securing their future prospects, and the festivals go late into the night. Time stands still in those wedding feasts and ceremonies. The excited yet patient anticipation for the bride is only overtaken by the groom, who is always late because tradition dictates that someone hide his shoe or another part of his wedding garb. Joyful pranks set the stage to prepare the couple for the unpredictable and the unexpected. But, amidst the joyful celebration and preparation for the unexpected, there is a serious note. Marriage is about long-term commitment.

Psalm 45 is no ordinary wedding song. It is a royal wedding song. There is a sense of joy and celebration, and there is also an element of seriousness. Stretching out the sceptre or strapping on a sword is most certainly a for-better-or-worse moment. But there is an even more serious note: there is that understanding that the throne of the king must prevail forever. This psalm calls to mind the church as the bride of Christ. She is preparing to serve and adore her King. Hers is the place of honor. Her King is preparing to give his life for her and not forfeit or abdicate his throne. It is his joyous task to be present with his bride. He will undertake great exploits in her name. The king will be elevated and esteemed, and the bride will participate in the victory processions.

I read this psalm in light of the text of the ten virgins in Matthew 25. There is preparation and waiting. The one who will arrive comes to be with the bride—the Immanuel, the present one, the protector, the provider, the promise keeper. This psalm highlights the single fact that the saviour of the church comes to receive unto himself the church for which he has given his life and will give his life (Ephesians

5:25–27). He is the Hosea to the church's Gomer, the redeemer of the unfaithful woman, yet still he rescues her and changes her identity and image into his likeness.

The Lord loves the church. He gave his life up for the church. No one can bring a charge against that which is in Christ Jesus (Romans 8:33–34). There is no condemnation against what Jesus has redeemed (Romans 8:1). Christ justified the church. In this psalm, I choose to see myself in the role of the servants who prepare the bride for the king's arrival. Seizing the opportunity and ascending the throne is not by chance for the redeeming Saviour. Jesus is the Redeemer of the church for the ages to come. All of the ceremony and the best outcomes, not just for the wedding but also for the marriage, are about preparation. Ultimately, preparation is what wins the victory at Calvary for all eternity. Are we ready for the moment when the bridegroom arrives?

QUESTIONS FOR REFLECTION OR DISCUSSION

1. The Bible speaks about the church as the bride of Christ. According to Ephesians 5:25–27, how does the bride prepare for the arrival of the groom?

    _____

    _____

    _____

2. How should we understand the ancient texts and the way they present the preparation of the church for eternity with Christ?

    _____

    _____

    _____

    _____

3. How are we to understand "condemnation" (Romans 8:1) and "separation" (Romans 8:35)?

    _____

    _____

    _____

    _____

PRAYER

Lord our God, thank you for seeking us out. We were lost and separated from you. Condemned by our own actions and empty of hope, we were foreigners. You, Lord, came to seek us out and gave us your identity. We are so glad your redeeming love acted on our behalf, and now we stand as part of your redeemed church. We join the Spirit and the bride and say, "Come Lord Jesus, come quickly." Amen.

DAY 25

WEDNESDAY

ONCE FOR ALL

SCRIPTURE

HEBREWS 10:4–10

For it is impossible for the blood of bulls and goats to take away sins. And it is by God's will that we have been sanctified through the offering of the body of Jesus Christ once for all.

—HEBREWS 10:4, 10

Early one Resurrection morning, the church gathered on the terrace gardens in the chilled morning air as part of our traditional sunrise and baptism service that would be followed by a fish braai. A fish braai is a traditional way of cooking fish on open coals of fire, similar to Jesus's style of preparing breakfast on the shores of the lake in John's Gospel (see John 21). As I concluded the open-air sermon, a group of approximately five people from the neighbourhood, dressed in religious gear that identified them as belonging to another religion than our own, approached me.

With little patience the group tore into the morning excitement for fellowship with rebukes and harsh words. "How dare you make noise so early in the morning?" Taken aback, I explained that we always cleared our church's intentions with the authorities before the sunrise service. I also explained that preaching on the grounds of the church was allowed as part of the South African culture of religious diversity. Again I heard: "Your message was about blood and more blood, and then you talked about the empty grave. Our children are not used to such things!" I noticed a gentleman who stood with the group but remained quiet in the one-sided fracas.

I turned to address him. "Sir, you have made the sacrifice to join us quite early this morning. It strikes me that you are accustomed to the early-morning sacrifice of religious service. You know that each morning you, along with many in your religious community, make the sacrifice of the morning call to prayer. It comes to us all via the loudspeakers on the minarets of the mosque. It is the call to pray that is broadcast not only in the mornings but five times throughout day. We in this church do not gather on your grounds to condemn that as noise."

The man responded to the members of his group: "The man of God is speaking the truth. We do this daily. This church only does so once a year."

I proceeded to reason with the gentleman that, while we talk about sacrifice and blood, "you offer the lives of bulls and sheep in blood offerings publicly. Perhaps we need to understand that the power of sacrifice is not simply in giving an animal's life. Our real sacrifice is in finding space and grace for each other and in offering the hard work of physical listening and reasoning together. As followers of Christ, we accept that Jesus has made the sacrifice of life and blood once for all so that we may find peace and offer his peace to others."

The gentleman stretched out his hand without another word, and I shook his hand and invited them to stay for fellowship. They graciously apologised and walked away in conversation with each other.

On Monday afternoon, the gentleman was in the church yard again, this time with his little son, using the long flat driveway of the church parking lot to teach the boy how to ride his bike.

QUESTIONS FOR REFLECTION OR DISCUSSION

1.   How do we sacrifice our lives to God today?

_____

_____

_____

_____

2.   How do we, like Jesus, sacrifice our lives for the sake of others?

_____

_____

_____

_____

3.   Later in Hebrews, in chapter 13, the author refers to a sacrifice of praise offered to God. What is a sacrifice of praise?

_____

_____

_____

_____

PRAYER

Now may the God of peace, who brought back from the dead our Lord Jesus, the great shepherd of the sheep, by the blood of the eternal covenant, make you complete in everything good so that you may do his will, working among us that which is pleasing in his sight, through Jesus Christ, to whom be the glory forever and ever. Amen.
(Hebrews 13:20–21)

DAY 26

THURSDAY

NOTHING WILL BE IMPOSSIBLE WITH GOD

SCRIPTURE

LUKE 1:26–38

The angel said to her, "Do not be afraid, Mary, for you have found favor with God. And now, you will conceive in your womb and bear a son, and you will name him Jesus." Mary said to the angel, "How can this be, since I am a virgin?" The angel said to her, "The Holy Spirit will come upon you, and the power of the Most High will overshadow you; therefore the child to be born will be holy; he will be called Son of God. For nothing will be impossible with God."

—LUKE 1:30–31, 34–35, 37

Often when I am overwhelmed and my thoughts are insufficient to understand the brokenness around me, I have to fall to my knees and connect to the triune conversation. There I am reassured by the Spirit of our God that he is present when life and its tasks seem impossible.

About two thousand years ago, a young girl was called to an impossible task. Mary was given the task of bringing the long-awaited Christ into this world. Mary asked, "How can this be?" She was a young woman who was not biologically, physically, or emotionally prepared for the task that God presented to her as a divine assignment. She was not even prepared socially in marriage when the call came to her. "How can this be?" is the kind of question that surfaces as an alternative to "What is going on here?"

It is not unusual for us to deal with tough assignments by asking questions. Often in my quest to fully understand my assignment I seek answers in conversation with so many other colleagues and friends that it becomes truly confusing due to the varied opinions on complex issues. On one hand, I know that different views can add perspective, but discernment for the right advisor or mentor is of critical importance for fuel on the journey. In today's text, Mary also helps me to see that it is imperative to seek clarity from God in moments of a critical collapse of understanding. The angel told Mary that the Holy Spirit would accomplish the task because "nothing is impossible with God."

You may be going through a tough season. Perhaps you are dealing with a difficult decision. Maybe you are wrestling with God on an assignment, or you are fighting an ailment. God is with you. How can this be? How will God do this? Remember, God is able to do the impossible. The Holy Spirit is sufficient. God's Holy Spirit will cleanse you. God's Holy Spirit will fill you. God's Holy Spirit will strengthen you. He gave the promise to Mary, and he gives it to you: God believes in you to carry this assignment to full term.

QUESTIONS FOR REFLECTION OR DISCUSSION

1. How are you praying right now concerning the size of your life assignment?

_____

_____

_____

_____

_____

_____

2. What is your life assignment from God?

_____

_____

_____

_____

_____

_____

PRAYER

Lord, you invite us to the assignments of our lives. Give peace to our hearts as we seek to know the details. Allow us to rest in the promise that the Holy Spirit will accomplish the things that seem impossible. Use us, Lord, as you see appropriate. Amen.

DAY 27
FRIDAY
THAT THEY MAY LIVE

SCRIPTURE

EZEKIEL 37:1-14

The hand of the LORD came upon me, and he brought me out by the spirit of the LORD and set me down in the middle of a valley; it was full of bones. He led me all around them; there were very many lying in the valley, and they were very dry. Then he said to me, "Prophesy to the breath, prophesy, mortal, and say to the breath: Thus says the Lord GOD: Come from the four winds, O breath, and breathe upon these slain, that they may live." I prophesied as he commanded me, and the breath came into them, and they lived, and stood on their feet, a vast multitude.

—EZEKIEL 37:1-2, 9-10

Could it be that the bones in today's text were a mighty military moving through the valley when, for some reason, they were killed? It may be that the army was not buried on the same day according to Jewish custom because the civilians the army protected were also killed. So in this passage, the shame of not being buried in death is reversed. The army is brought back to life. There is a promise given to all who believe in Jesus that we shall not die but have eternal life. The mighty people of God will not lie in shame, "cut off completely."

We have an echo of this text in Acts: "Suddenly a sound like the blowing of a violent wind came from heaven and filled the whole house where they were sitting. They saw what seemed to be tongues of fire that separated and came to rest on each of them. All of them were filled with the Holy Spirit and began to speak in other tongues as the Spirit enabled them" (2:2–4, NIV). The Creator God brings the vision of the promise of new life in Ezekiel 37: God breathes upon the dried bones, and they come back to life as a mighty army. Jesus, through the Holy Spirit, breathes on his disciples in Acts, and ever since then, the church has been an army of light bearers, carrying light into a darkened world. We have become a mighty army of the kingdom of light. As we seek the Holy Spirit deeply, God fills our lives, cleansing us and breathing within us a whole heart of love that displaces death and separation and restores personal and collective wholeness. The bones do not arise as *only* individuals. We arise as God's collective. Love is the power of the army of God.

The Spirit assures us that our mortal bodies will be empowered with strength and life. God has invited you and me into the Spirit-filled life. Let us ask him to give us his Spirit. Let us come before him in faith. Let us pray, admitting that we need him, more than ever before. Let us believe that only he can satisfy our spiritual hunger. Let us confess him as the only true leader of our lives. Daily pursue him in deep prayer until you are filled with new love and new life. Pray that you will encounter God in a way that will totally transform you, and pray that his love remains within you forever.

Let's speak those words of life and witness into the church. Let's sing them over again and again. We must bear witness to the works of God in the present season. Like Moses and the burning bush, Elijah on Mt. Carmel, and the disciples in the upper room, may we relate our holy encounters with the divine, bearing witness to the indwelling power and reality of the Holy Spirit. God gives himself freely to us as a gift. Just like good earthly dads desire to bless their children, so does our heavenly Father choose to bless us with a transformation story too good to pass up the opportunity to live again each time it is told.

QUESTIONS FOR REFLECTION OR DISCUSSION

1. When was the last time you heard a fresh, transforming story of
    how God raised up someone from a valley experience? When last
    did you see that story lived out in a community?

    _____

    _____

    _____

    _____

    _____

    _____

2. How can we be obedient like Ezekiel was, to prophesy and
    trust that God will bring about new life for our churches and
    communities?

    _____

    _____

    _____

    _____

    _____

    _____

PRAYER

*Lord, we come to you in expectation. We desire to attempt greater things
for you, Lord God. We expect greater things from you, God of Abraham,
Isaac, and Jacob. God of Moses, Elijah, and all the apostles,
fill us with your Spirit again and again. Lord, our God,
we know you will not disappoint. Amen.*

DAY 28

SATURDAY

IN YOUR STEADFAST LOVE

SCRIPTURE

PSALM 31:9-16

Be gracious to me, O Lord, for I am in distress; my eye wastes away from grief, my soul and body also. For my life is spent with sorrow, and my years with sighing; my strength fails because of my misery, and my bones waste away. For I hear the whispering of many—terror all around!—as they scheme together against me, as they plot to take my life. But I trust in you, O Lord; I say, "You are my God." My times are in your hand; deliver me from the hand of my enemies and persecutors. Let your face shine upon your servant; save me in your steadfast love.

—PSALM 31:9-10, 13-16

"Rock bottom." These two words seem to best describe this psalm of disorientation. We know the psalms formed part of the ancient liturgies in synagogues and devotional times, but I can't imagine using one like this in Sunday worship. I cannot imagine someone reminding me of a painful time of illness and disease, compounded with depression and discouragement. I believe the threats and lies from the enemies the psalmist mentions have led to the deep soul sickness described in this text. The sickness that almost caused death is certainly physiological, and it may be a case of mind over matter—or, rather, mind affecting matter. Whatever the case was, the writer was sick to the bones and his eyes sealed shut from the thick, consistent, feverish tears flowing in a time of death and disease.

Have you ever been as sick as that? No doubt many reading this have suffered deep afflictions of discouragement and disease. I know I have on more than one occasion. As a missionary who has frequently travelled through the African continent, I became frighteningly ill on a number of occasions. Sickness that leaps upon one without warning is the worst kind. A few years ago I lost my younger brother to such an illness. It was a little under a week that he was ill, and then he suddenly died. There was no way any of us could prepare for such a permanent outcome of what seemed at first to be nothing. Sudden sickness and disease leaves a gaping wound, causing us to wonder, *What just happened? What did I miss?*

I believe in divine healing. Seldom have I witnessed instantaneous healing like I did one night in my college dorm room. I was ill from a bacterial infection contracted from water I had consumed. Struck down with deep pain, locked down in my room, I prayed hard and fell asleep. I thought my life would end that night in my college dorm. Once asleep, I experienced a beautiful encounter. It is not possible to tell whether it was a dream or partial reality, but when I awoke in the morning, I was completely healed.

I do not know why all prayers for healing do not have the same results. I do not believe it is a measurable quantity of faith or eloquence of prayer that heals. All I know is that, after two and a half decades of praying for healing for people and at times asking God for the impossible, I have seen that in the end, love never fails. I am convinced that fervent prayers of righteous people and divine healing both flow from a place of love. God heals some instantly; others are healed progressively. I have heard it said that instant healing is good for testimony while progressive healing is good for relationship-building. Either way, love never fails. Some may ask, "What about those who died waiting to be healed?" I truly do not have an answer. I prayed in the days when my brother was so sick. I was so desperate that I asked God to cash up all my ministry service days and turn them into some kind of heavenly currency for healing. But my brother died. I remain in the hope that, even there, love never failed.

In the final lines of the sad Psalm 31, there is a glimmer of hope that love never fails. It reaches into eternity and strengthens our hope. We are led to the rock that is higher than us all.

QUESTIONS FOR REFLECTION OR DISCUSSION

1. What do you believe about divine healing?

2. How do you see the relationship between God's love and divine healing?

3. What does death for a saint in this life mean?

PRAYER

Blessed be the LORD, for he has wondrously shown his steadfast love to me when I was beset as a city under siege. I had said in my alarm, "I am driven far from your sight." But you heard my supplications when I cried out to you for help. Love the LORD, all you his saints. The LORD preserves the faithful, but abundantly repays the one who acts haughtily. Be strong, and let your heart take courage, all you who wait for the LORD.
—Psalm 31:21–24

FIFTH
SUNDAY
IN LENT

THE LORD IS GRACIOUS
AND MERCIFUL

SCRIPTURE

PSALM 145

The LORD is gracious and merciful, slow to anger and abounding in
steadfast love. The LORD is good to all, and his compassion is over all that
he has made. The LORD is faithful in all his words, and gracious in all his
deeds. The LORD upholds all who are falling, and raises up all who are
bowed down. The LORD is just in all his ways, and kind in
all his doings. The LORD is near to all who call on him, to all who
call on him in truth. He fulfills the desire of all who fear him;
he also hears their cry, and saves them.

—PSALM 145:8–9, 13b–14, 17–19

On the journey of life there will be marriage and birth, living and dying, sickness and health. Life will serve at its table disillusionment and disappointment, and certainly there will be laughter. The sun, however, will rise again each tomorrow. Tomorrow we will discover new orientation. Psalm 145 is written as an acrostic in Hebrew. Each verse begins with a new letter of the Hebrew alphabet, suggesting that each line covers some aspect of the fullness of God in our lives. Each tomorrow brings resurrection hope and its possibilities. In each verse there is grace for a new day. There is no part of our lives in which God is not involved. He is always good and always present.

This psalm speaks to several beautiful things about living in relationship to God. The first two verses are about daily choices. Before the disclosure and the revelation of who God is, the psalmist declares his intent to praise and worship God. It is wonderful to be able to trust God in this way. I can't help but wonder if our human nature may be inclined to ask, *What is the benefit for me in all of this? How will I get the maximum before I give my bare minimum?* We all tend to be concerned with "what's in it for me." I get the feeling in these verses that the writer is saying he commits his all to God before he even fully accepts the unknown abundance in God. It's a commitment that says: *I signed up with you forever. My decision is made. I will serve you.* It feels similar to a marriage commitment. In cultures with Middle Eastern practices, commitment is the bedrock of relationships. The walls represent trust while love is the roof, but the foundation remains commitment. For the psalmist, the decision to rest on commitment has been settled. Modern society tends to leave a backdoor clause for a walkout. No relationship can survive half-hearted commitment. Here the psalmist communicates that he thinks the utmost of God and declares his commitment before he even unpacks all of the goodness of God. Once we make the decision to love Jesus, all other decisions are easier. We work from that place of for Christ or against him. Love and commitment form the basis of decision-making.

Next, the psalmist discloses who God is. In this segment I get the feeling the psalmist desires to tell us all the reasons he would never let go of the Lord's hand. The grace on each level expressed as "compassion" in verse 8, down to God being watchful and vigilant over God's children in verse 20, is ultimately exemplified in Jesus our Saviour and incarnate God. This is the full disclosure of the nature and character of God. Having seen and experienced Christ, we have come to know who God is.

Finally, the psalmist describes God as deliverer. He is the one who restores the lost relationship of the garden. After four hundred years of silence, Jesus arrives and breaks the silence, reconciling humanity to God and becoming the language of God's love.

Our response cannot end in simply receiving all the abundant grace that God bestows. The restoration that comes from God restores our position at the table. Humanity along with all other creatures enjoy the esteemed place. In Christ, we are restored to full authority. We are given the promise of all eternity, and we now walk with new integrity. That which is merely clay now occupies the highest place of response to God. We sit at the table with him in the midst of enemies.

QUESTIONS FOR REFLECTION OR DISCUSSION

1. Who is Jesus in your life?

_____

_____

_____

_____

2. How or when have you experienced God's full disclosure of his grace, mercy, love, and compassion in your life?

_____

_____

_____

_____

3. How can we fully commit ourselves to God, even without fully understanding God's ways?

_____

_____

_____

_____

_____

PRAYER

Lord, in this part of the journey, help us to give you our trust and love long before we explore what is in it for us. We love you, and it does not matter what this life may hold. May we only concern ourselves with who holds our lives! Amen.

DAY 29
MONDAY
THAT IS MY NAME

SCRIPTURE

ISAIAH 42:1–9

I am the Lord, I have called you in righteousness, I have taken you by the hand and kept you; I have given you as a covenant to the people, a light to the nations, to open the eyes that are blind, to bring out the prisoners from the dungeon, from the prison those who sit in darkness. I am the Lord, that is my name; my glory I give to no other, nor my praise to idols. See, the former things have come to pass, and new things I now declare; before they spring forth, I tell you of them.

—ISAIAH 42:6–9

Owning our names is fundamental to our identity. In the ancient world, the name was a clear descriptor of the character and nature of a person. As a South African, I can relate to this attitude toward names. I had a friend called Wiseman in the village where I grew up. It was evident that he truly was wise. A lot of what he did reflected patience in conversation, and he exuded a grace and peace that made him winsome. In school he came first in most things.

Indulge me as I bear witness to the ways of God. I did not always know why I was given the name Gabriel. Long after I responded to my call to ministry, my mum told me the story of how I received my name. She told me of a missionary serving in what was known as the Dutch Reformed Church in Durban. He did something unconventional for his faith tradition: he prayed for my mum, who was pregnant with me. He spoke (as my mum describes) with a prophetic sharpness. He said to my mum that the one she was carrying would grow to be a preacher. He offered the name Stephan, an Afrikaans version of the name Stephen. My mum did not like that name and said she preferred Gabriel. Mum said to me with her wit, "Even though I was a new Christian at that point, I did not wish to martyr you." She insisted that I would live to proclaim the Lord.

I did not at first know that was how I received my name. I wrestled with spiritual battles as a youth, and following and serving God was far from my mind. I was a curious learner and avid reader. Helpful and healthy information was not always readily available. I was tempted at many points to turn toward atheism. Three years into my theological studies, my mum told me, "You were identified as a preacher even before you were born. God had his hand upon you, and all I wanted to do was pray and watch God fulfill his promise." So here I am as Gabriel, one whose name means "God is my strength." It seems to fit a preacher because the angel Gabriel was a messenger from God. I cannot say biblical names will always yield the fruit of their meanings, but God clearly used my name to illustrate and affirm my calling.

God is true to his own name. In describing himself to Moses, God revealed that he is all sufficient for the cause: "I AM WHO I AM" (Exodus 3:14). God cannot be unfaithful to his name. Essentially, God is truth and will not break his own reality. As God, he chooses to remain true to his word. God's name is not what he *aspires* to be. God's name is who God *is*. There is no error in God's thinking about who he is. He is *Elohim*—God. He is *El Shaddai*—God Almighty. He is *Elyon*—God Most High. He is *Adonai*—Lord God. In Christ God is the *Logos*—Word. God is *Jehovah Sabaoth*—God of the host of heavenly armies. God is *Jireh*—the one who will provide. God is the name above all names.

The list of God's names is far more than I have offered here, yet still this paltry list proves the point that God is love and will be our sufficiency in every circumstance. When I read this Isaiah text, I am filled with the promise and hope that, if God can offer me a name to live into, then he has called us collectively by his name. We are his brand ambassadors, as David said: "He leads me in right paths for his name's sake" (Psalm 23:3). As you reflect on his name, know that God promised long ago that he would crush the enemy under the foot of a Saviour. God kept his promise since the beginning in the very name of Jesus—"the one who saves us."

QUESTIONS FOR REFLECTION OR DISCUSSION

1. If we are called by God's name, how do we live out the truth in his name?

    _____

    _____

    _____

    _____

    _____

    _____

2. If God's name is above all other names, then that should include the names of our diseases and troubles. How can we bring all other names under his name?

    _____

    _____

    _____

    _____

    _____

    _____

    _____

PRAYER

Lord, our God. You do not deny who you are. You do not hide your eternal reality from us. You never betray the names by which we have come to know you. We cry out, "Abba. Father. Our Prince of Peace!" You are our Lord and Saviour. Remain Lord over our lives, and let your name be greater than all the names we bring in subjection to you. Amen.

DAY 30
TUESDAY
A GRAIN OF WHEAT

SCRIPTURE

JOHN 12:20–36

Jesus answered them, "The hour has come for the Son of Man
to be glorified. Very truly, I tell you, unless a grain of wheat falls into
the earth and dies, it remains just a single grain; but if it dies, it bears much
fruit. Those who love their life lose it, and those who hate their life in this
world will keep it for eternal life. Whoever serves me must follow me,
and where I am, there will my servant be also. Whoever serves me,
the Father will honor. Now my soul is troubled. And what
should I say—'Father, save me from this hour'? No, it is
for this reason that I have come to this hour."

—*JOHN 12:23–27*

A single grain of wheat in itself falling to the ground seems insignificant. Zimbabwe was once proudly known as the bread basket of Africa. Wheat was Zimbabwe's major commercial product. The wheat plantations teach us a deep truth. The dropping of grain to the floor is not a matter of chance. A careful farmer works behind the scenes to ensure sustainability. The wheat extracted for milling is the wheat the public consumes as flour. The flour becomes bread. The careful farmer not only plants for the milling process but also grows a certain percentage of crop to sustain future crops. Some wheat is sown as grain back into the soil so that the food supply remains secure.

Paul talks about generous sowing, reaping, and having seed for sustainability in the next season (2 Corinthians 9:6–11). The idea behind a single grain of wheat dying is that it will rise again with greater potential. The grain must first fall out of the head of wheat. That is a singular journey to the earth. The earth will cover it and unlock the power of the seed in order for a whole new plant to grow. In doing so, what follows is the exponential power of growth and life.

Jesus demonstrated this truth in the most real and living way. In all things, we see the principle of multiplication. Something gives its life in order for many more to live. In the breaking down of bread, our souls are nourished so that many more receive the gospel of truth through us. In the crushing of the grape, the thirst of many is quenched. Jesus talked about the act of eating the life-giving bread and drinking of the thirst-quenching cup in order to fully experience life. He wasn't talking about reincarnation. He meant that the life of usefulness and significance is built into every one of us. As has been stated innumerable times, one can count the seeds in an apple, but no one can count the apples in a seed. The potential to transform life that is trapped within a seed cannot be fully quantified.

Followers of Christ carry great transformational potential within us. The gifts that shape our identities are sufficient to change the world. As followers of Christ, we choose to be partakers of his life and be built up in him, through him, and by him so that in the same way Christ offered himself we too bring forth a joyful willingness to transform and be transformed—to become consumed by the idea of giving up life to give life. Jesus lived out every aspect of this teaching with his life and willing death. Living wheat is good to eat. A grain that dies multiplies.

QUESTIONS FOR REFLECTION OR DISCUSSION

1. What do you believe is the ultimate cost of being a witness for Christ?

2. In the New Testament, the Greek word from which we derive our English word "martyr" is a word that means "witness." How does this knowledge change how you view what it means for Christians to be martyrs? What is the relationship between being a witness and being a martyr?

3. What role does willingness play in the life of a follower of Christ?

PRAYER

Father, you have called us to live for your glory. You invite us daily to lay down our lives so that we too may fearlessly live again in power of the gospel. We are your children. Let your life shine brightly in and through us, that others may see the power of your transforming love that will raise us back in greater purpose and number. Amen.

DAY 31
WEDNESDAY
SINCE WE ARE SURROUNDED

SCRIPTURE

HEBREWS 12:1-4

Therefore, since we are surrounded by so great a cloud of witnesses, let us also lay aside every weight and the sin that clings so closely, and let us run with perseverance the race that is set before us, looking to Jesus the pioneer and perfecter of our faith, who for the sake of the joy that was set before him endured the cross, disregarding its shame, and has taken his seat at the right hand of the throne of God. Consider him who endured such hostility against himself from sinners, so that you may not grow weary or lose heart. In your struggle against sin you have not yet resisted to the point of shedding your blood.

—HEBREWS 12:1-4

So much of what we do today is dependent on finding truth and truth-seeking. We have seen the ready and desperate need in the season of the pandemic for a clear and useful distinction of facts and truth from perceptions and opinions. Daily lived out pressure and challenges bore down to the core of truth. South Africa has fairly recently experienced events that erupted into violent demonstrations that led to great distress and even death because of the opinions and lawless perspectives of leaders who incited racial discord and hatred. If each person embraced the truth that sets humanity free, the way forward would be peaceful.

Truth works on our internal design. As image bearers of God, we have a spiritual bias toward the magnetic north of truth. Those ancients who bore witness to truth and arrived at the exact coordinates now stand as our cloud of witnesses. These witnesses have left the substance of our hope and the evidence of things not yet seen (Hebrews 11:1–2). We are those who follow behind them; experiencing the evidence and the substance of their journey encourages us to stay on track. Truth has a sense of connectedness to the witnesses from our past. As we follow closely, we stay on track in order to arrive at the same place—that better, heavenly country (Hebrews 11:16). The witnesses have set their footprints in the Way, the Truth, and the Life. With their footprints before us, let us run with endurance, being mindful of their steps.

The particular race that is before us is not a competition against others. The race has a particular way of encouraging us to accomplish all that God has set before us. We are simply to follow the track that will always bring us to what is good. In our race, the intrinsic worth of each step is in itself a spiritual discovery. We find that the life encounters and experiences of all faith heroes, like Moses and Rahab, have great worth for us in our practice. Exploring the lifestyles of the champions like Abraham, Sarah, and Samson reveals deep and fetching diversity in their relationships with God. The one common experience they all share is that each one believed in and trusted God. Truth untangles our feet from the sin that so easily befalls us.

As boys, we found great pleasure in playing on the South African *bushveld* in a place called Mariannhill. The veld is another name for open spaces populated with a range of tough grass and durable plants. The common grass is thatch grass, used now in roofing luxury homes. One thing I learned was that if one tied a tuft of thatch grass across a pathway to another tuft on the other side of the pathway, it was strong enough to drop a friend, or even a donkey, or both. We ran along the pathways to school and back, and Fridays were careful days because of the tricksters who tied the grass that so easily tripped us. The lesser-worn pathways made spotting the traps difficult. If the people of God follow closely in the well-used pathways of prayer, holiness, faith, and grace of those who walked before us, the traps become easier to spot and avoid.

Safe journeys to you who walk the way of the Lord in the pathways of the saints who have gone ahead of us. There have been many who made their way before us. They walked and ran with endurance. Though at times some may have fallen, they got up and continued to run with endurance the race set before them. May we do the same. Run with great perseverance.

QUESTIONS FOR REFLECTION OR DISCUSSION

1. How can you spot and avoid the thatch grass (points of sin, temptation, and error) that is knotted along a believer's pathway?

2. How can travelling this journey with others help us spot traps?

3. How can we untangle traps we find so that those coming up behind us may more easily overcome the things that may hinder their journey?

PRAYER

Lord, you are a faithful Shepherd. You lead us in green pathways, and you help guide us into the clearest route forward. Help us not to give up. Help us persevere even when we stumble. May we not be fearful of getting up to keep going forward. Amen.

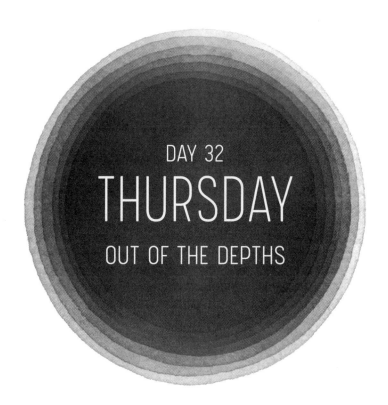

DAY 32
THURSDAY
OUT OF THE DEPTHS

SCRIPTURE

PSALM 130

Out of the depths I cry to you, O Lord. Lord, hear my voice! Let your ears be attentive to the voice of my supplications! If you, O Lord, should mark iniquities, Lord, who could stand? But there is forgiveness with you, so that you may be revered. I wait for the Lord, my soul waits, and in his word I hope; my soul waits for the Lord more than those who watch for the morning, more than those who watch for the morning. O Israel, hope in the Lord! For with the Lord there is steadfast love, and with him is great power to redeem. It is he who will redeem Israel from all its iniquities.

—PSALM 130

The people of God often turn to Psalms when we need scriptural encouragement. I served as a bedside-attending pastor for many years. I have held the hands of many people as they reached out in spirit and opened the door to the other side. On a few occasions I have witnessed patients who have had a complete loss of mind and faculty still look at me with wide-eyed wonder when I read from the book of Psalms. I still cannot fully comprehend why, when I recited Psalm 23 or other popular psalms to people who were completely out of mind, they recited along with me with deep conviction and peace. New life and new hope come from the Word of God. I go to Psalms when I want to feel like someone out there knows my struggle. Psalms connects me to my deepest human struggles, and it often points me to solutions.

Walter Brueggemann suggests that we have a love-hate relationship with Psalms. On one hand, we may enjoy reciting our favourite psalms while on the other we carefully edit some verses out because they make us uncomfortable. Some portions are brutal, while other pieces are contagiously memorable. Brueggemann says we can broadly categorize the psalms into psalms of orientation, disorientation, and reorientation—or what I like to call generation (first things, or beginnings), degeneration (atrophy and destruction), and regeneration (a fusion response to first things and formation of new things).

We identify with the psalms because they speak to the seasons of our lives. There are beginnings, there are changes and endings, and then there are new beginnings. Genesis reveals the creation of all things in a season of generation. Then comes the fall of humanity, a time of degeneration (or disorientation), and thereafter came the promise of a new normal—*euangelion* in the Greek, which means "gospel;" new life in the promised Saviour; regeneration. These seasons of our lives also play out clearly in the life of Jesus, from his birth (generation) to his death (degeneration) and then his resurrection (regeneration).

Psalm 130 starts with disorientation, or degeneration, and moves to reorientiation, or regeneration. When the air gets thin, the psalm breathes new life into the sojourner. This psalm is a powerful reminder of the depths we could sink to without God. It is also refreshing to learn that God comes into the depths of hopelessness to free us from the isolating power of sin. Psalm 130 highlights the destructive, dislocating pain that sin brings into our relationships. Sin alienates us from our Creator. Sin throws a person deep into loss of purpose and reality. The feelings of disorientation, degradation, and degeneration are isolating and overwhelming.

The psalmist then reminds us of the reorientation and new life that are available to us in the Spirit. There's a new day coming. Our hope is that, beyond disorientation, there is new orientation. Our peace comes from knowing that, beyond degeneration, there is regeneration. After death comes resurrection. The psalm concludes by saying that, even though iniquities have destroyed our normal lives, God is making all things new again and again.

QUESTIONS FOR REFLECTION OR DISCUSSION

1. What season are you in? A season of beginnings, endings, or new beginnings?

   _____

   _____

   _____

   _____

2. How do you sense the presence of the Lord?

   _____

   _____

   _____

   _____

3. How does this psalm help you know that new beginnings are on the horizon?

   _____

   _____

   _____

   _____

   _____

PRAYER

Lord Jesus, thank you for framing our lives in yours. From the normal to the broken to the promise of new life, it all makes sense when we see the empty tomb. Life in you ends in triumph, and we rest in that promise.
Amen.

DAY 33
FRIDAY
SET THE MIND ON THE SPIRIT

SCRIPTURE

ROMANS 8:1-11

To set the mind on the flesh is death, but to set the mind on the Spirit is life and peace. For this reason the mind that is set on the flesh is hostile to God; it does not submit to God's law—indeed it cannot, and those who are in the flesh cannot please God. But you are not in the flesh; you are in the Spirit, since the Spirit of God dwells in you. Anyone who does not have the Spirit of Christ does not belong to him. But if Christ is in you, though the body is dead because of sin, the Spirit is life because of righteousness. If the Spirit of him who raised Jesus from the dead dwells in you, he who raised Christ from the dead will give life to your mortal bodies also through his Spirit that dwells in you.

—ROMANS 8:6-11

My parents raised four sons, all approximately two years apart. I cannot remember a day growing up when my mum was not applying a disinfectant to a wound, wiping off blood, applying a bandage, or threatening to punish one or all of us while slipping in a prayer for healing and added strength. As brothers, we were a tight band, like a fist of fingers. My younger brother Herman and I were the middle two. It was generally accepted that he was the handsomest, brightest, and most athletic among us all. Herman had something about him that was saturated in explorative mischief; wherever Herman was, there was the spirit of adventure, always accompanied by a mischievous smile.

One morning during the winter holidays, in the cold dusty grounds of Mariannhill, Herman stood barefoot beside our older brother's new yellow chopper bike. My younger brother taught me how to mount a bike and race those balloon tyres on the soft, white "moon dust." We rode fast and furiously to make the most of the hour or so of the "borrowed" bicycle before its owner awakened. On that chilly morning, Herman and I flew down the hills as fast as his nine-year-old legs could generate speed. We arrived at a spot that was fairly flat and freshly cleared, where a farmer would grow the mustard flower used in the Hindu temples. In the middle of the clearing was a huge tree stump. Herman pushed me around the field, and as I gained the courage and momentum to sit upright he said, "Do not hit the stump."

From that moment, my mind could think of nothing else but the tree stump. I was doing well and then found myself gathering speed, and I looked at the stump. Then I hit the stump. The buckled front rim and the shocked look of horror on Herman's face taught me one of the great lessons of my life: what our minds fixate on becomes a magnetic centre. Perhaps the Proverbs writer captured it by saying: "For as he thinks within himself, so he is" (Proverbs 23:7, NASB). In our scripture for today, Paul uses the words "to set the mind on the flesh." The word in the Greek for mindset is *phroneo*. Scholars tend to agree that it means "a frame of mind"—that frame which sets itself around the object of our attention. Paul reminds us that we are no longer in the flesh. In the Spirit, we have a new frame of mind, and ought to develop the discipline of relating to God in the Spirit.

Before she converted to Christianity, my mum practiced an Eastern religion. She testifies that, prior to becoming aware of salvation in Christ, she and her family were constantly focused on surviving the physical world. Their gods were servants who helped deal with the fears of day-to-day living. Fear drove her religious pursuit. In the Holy Spirit, "perfect love casts out fear" (1 John 4:18). Life in the Spirit overcomes fear by trusting and understanding the ways of God (1 Corinthians 2:12).

In today's text, Paul says that those who are in Christ are not in the flesh. We ought not to be people who claim to have knowledge of God and give way to satisfying the flesh. If our frame of mind is centered on God, then the depth of our thinking and living and loving will be a picture of a whole heart of love for God. The outworking of all our words, deeds, and actions will bring honour to God. The life in the Spirit is a constantly developing quality, moving away from being governed by fear and feelings and toward a life led by trust, love, and faith in the one who saves us.

QUESTIONS FOR REFLECTION OR DISCUSSION

1. What is your mind centered on?

_____

_____

_____

_____

_____

_____

_____

2. What do you go to bed thinking about, and what do you wake up thinking about?

_____

_____

_____

_____

_____

_____

_____

PRAYER

Lord Jesus, thank you for your great accomplishment on Calvary. So great a work for us was undertaken that it frames all the objects of our minds and hearts. Help us constantly set our minds on you. Keep us in perfect peace because our minds are fixed on you (Isaiah 26:3). Amen.

DAY 34
LAZARUS SATURDAY

I AM THE RESURRECTION AND THE LIFE

SCRIPTURE

JOHN 11:1-44

When Martha heard that Jesus was coming, she went and met him, while Mary stayed at home. Martha said to Jesus, "Lord, if you had been here, my brother would not have died. But even now I know that God will give you whatever you ask of him." Jesus said to her, "Your brother will rise again." Martha said to him, "I know that he will rise again in the resurrection on the last day." Jesus said to her, "I am the resurrection and the life. Those who believe in me, even though they die, will live, and everyone who lives and believes in me will never die. Do you believe this?" She said to him, "Yes, Lord, I believe that you are the Messiah, the Son of God, the one coming into the world."

—JOHN 11:20-27

Some call the day before Palm Sunday "Lazarus Saturday" to commemorate the day Jesus went to the town of Bethany because his friend Lazarus had fallen ill and died. A few days before visiting his friends—the siblings Martha, Mary, and Lazarus—in Bethany, Jesus received news that Lazarus was critically ill. As good sisters, Martha and Mary confidently sent word to ask Jesus to do what they knew was true about him. They knew he was a problem solver. They rested in the fact that he was a healer. Upon receiving the urgent invitation to attend to his sick friend, Jesus delayed his response by forty-eight hours, and then learned that Lazarus had died. Then Jesus made his way to Bethany.

Mary and Martha may have thought Jesus was careless to delay his journey. However they felt, these sisters were not going to be silent about the matter. "You let him die" was essentially their accusation. "You knew he was sick, and you allowed this. Lazarus is dead." The real question underlying their accusations may be best framed as, "Where were you when we needed you?"

People speak such words out of deep hurt and helplessness. Jesus, however, had a purpose. Martha demonstrated that she had a handle on a nascent theology of resurrection. For Jesus at that point, resurrection was not simply a matter of knowledge. Many people know things and still don't believe. Knowledge of resurrection was not evidence of belief. Resurrection is *Jesus*, and Jesus is the resurrection. The claim "I am the resurrection," like all of the "I am" sayings of Jesus in the Gospel of John, remains rooted in the reality of his person. To know him and to believe in him is to fully experience all that he is.

Jesus extended hope into the grip of the grave. It was not about him being selfish. It was about Jesus bringing forth explosive, dynamic belief. Establishing hope was the end goal. He did this by choosing to create the background for a miracle. Difficulty is not a sufficient backdrop for the impossible. Impossibility is the backdrop for a miracle. Join me in believing in Jesus, that we may fully experience him as resurrection and life even in the face of our greatest enemy, death.

QUESTIONS FOR REFLECTION OR DISCUSSION

1. What are some of the other "I am" sayings of Jesus in the Gospel of John? (See John 6:35; 8:12; 9:5; 10:7, 11; 14:6; 15:1.)

2. How can you relate to Martha and Mary in their anguish and sense of deflation in hope?

3. What does it mean for you to be called a "believer"?

4. How different is it to *know about* Jesus than to *believe in* Jesus?

PRAYER

Lord Jesus, we long to know you in a deep and eternal way.
Help our unbelief. Help us to receive you into our hearts and lives
that we may know you and fully experience you. Amen.

PALM SUNDAY

HOSANNA

SCRIPTURE

MATTHEW 21:1–11

The disciples went and did as Jesus had directed them; they brought the donkey and the colt, and put their cloaks on them, and he sat on them. A very large crowd spread their cloaks on the road, and others cut branches from the trees and spread them on the road. The crowds that went ahead of him and that followed were shouting, "Hosanna to the Son of David! Blessed is the one who comes in the name of the Lord! Hosanna in the highest heaven!" When he entered Jerusalem, the whole city was in turmoil, asking, "Who is this?" The crowds were saying, "This is the prophet Jesus from Nazareth in Galilee."

—*MATTHEW 21:6–11*

Holy Week lies before us. Look with me at love's triumphal entry. The generals and war heroes are coming in through the gates as they are called upon to strengthen security systems for Passover week. These celebrities from the war fronts are celebrated for their strategy and power to end lives, and they wear their war stripes with pride. Then there is that moment when one comes in the name of the Lord. Jesus is at the gate. This triumphant King does not take lives. Instead, he lays down his life in order to give life. In him is the true triumph over death. He reversed the curse of death, accomplishing what no one else could do. He restored the original order of the earth. He comes in humility to burst open the tombs and restore life. Who can stop the pent-up anticipation of creation's hope when such a king comes through the gates? Can the crowds be expected to remain silent? The military generals of war fade in glory in comparison to the arrival of the restorer of life.

With the same desire to contain the glorious love manifested as resurrection power that Peter demonstrated on the mount of trans-figuration, the enamoured crowds attempt to capture Jesus as a national hero. Riding in on a donkey on Palm Sunday, the crowd wants to crown him as their king. Theirs would be a glorious attempt to nationalise and localise God. Jesus squarely looks at the controlling spirits and silences them. He did not come to earth to lead one nation in its political pursuits. He was clear when he said, "My kingdom is not of this world" (John 18:36, NIV).

Jesus reminds his listeners that his call is not to a singular nationality, nor is his kingship of worldly power. Jesus came to rule in the hearts of children, women, and men who understand his higher call for us to be citizens of heaven and children of God. Let us come into this moment with deep gratitude. The Bethany event on Lazarus Saturday foretold of the abundant grace for everyone. Resurrection life is in the air. Let us also come into this moment with great reverence and care. Let us not turn our songs of joy and anticipation of life into something else in the days of Holy Week. Let us prepare our hearts for the moment of God that is coming in one week.

QUESTIONS FOR REFLECTION OR DISCUSSION

1. What does Palm Sunday mean to you?

_____

_____

_____

_____

2. The people who celebrated Jesus on Palm Sunday wanted to contain Jesus as a national hero. What did Jesus declare his purpose to be on earth?

_____

_____

_____

_____

3. How are you preparing to receive Christ again, afresh and anew, in your life this season?

_____

_____

_____

_____

PRAYER

Lord of all people and culture, we sing Hosanna! Blessed are you, Lord. Come and dwell within us. Glorify yourself through our lives. Use us to be missional and to represent your holiness, in order that we may reflect your grace as Christians in the world around us. Amen.

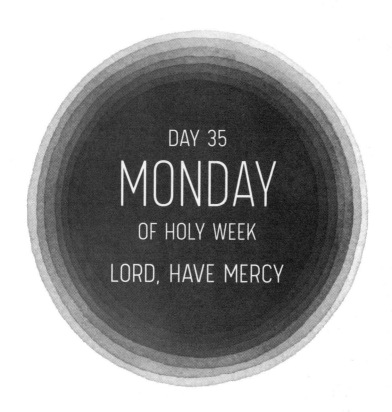

DAY 35

MONDAY

OF HOLY WEEK

LORD, HAVE MERCY

SCRIPTURE

MATTHEW 20:29–34

As they were leaving Jericho, a large crowd followed him.
There were two blind men sitting by the roadside. When they heard
that Jesus was passing by, they shouted, "Lord, have mercy on us,
Son of David!" Jesus stood still and called them, saying, "What do you want
me to do for you?" They said to him, "Lord, let our eyes be opened."
Moved with compassion, Jesus touched their eyes.
Immediately they regained their sight and followed him.

—MATTHEW 20:29–30, 32–34

Imagine a time in history when there was no efficiency in medicine and healthcare. It is difficult for us today to even think about a simple toothache or a persistent migraine without reaching for pain relief. Simply thinking about suffering, sickness, and pain today is a challenge, even with all the advanced technologies we have. Even though the very best of the world's experts and knowledge archives are present in our world, we have not become any more enlightened about how to deal with suffering and pain once and for all. If we consider ourselves enlightened, then why are we still heavy-hearted? With all of the best of the best things we possess, still here we are, waiting at the gates for a hero to pass by. Separated from possible solutions, healers, and heroes, we suffer in blinding darkness.

As Jesus began his journey into the holy city, before the events of pain and death met him personally in a duel for humankind's soul, he encountered many who painted with vivid colours our timeless and collective hopelessness. On his way toward Jerusalem, he finds the broken, blind men screaming out for wholeness. Theirs is a call for him to restore more than sight. It is the call of humankind to the only one who can restore wholeness—but not without resistance. When I was a boy, I dislocated my shoulder. The expert forcing back into place of two pieces of bone and cartilage that had once worked in complete harmony restored wholeness—but not without resistance and pain.

So Jesus began the week with his face set toward the point of resistance—Golgotha, that place where all the resistance of the forces keeping the world from wholeness would crumble. God was in him reconciling all things to himself. When I find myself at that point of greatest division and resistance, I know something good is about to happen. That which was dislocated and out of joint will once and for all be made whole again. Eyes are opened and vision is restored. They find mercy.

QUESTIONS FOR REFLECTION OR DISCUSSION

1. What causes you so much pain that it compels you to cry out?

_____

_____

_____

_____

_____

_____

_____

2. What gives you hope in the restoration of Jesus?

_____

_____

_____

_____

_____

_____

_____

PRAYER

Father God, work in us to keep us whole and holy.
We know that Christ is at work in us. Amen.

DAY 36

TUESDAY

OF HOLY WEEK

YOUR KING IS COMING

SCRIPTURE

MATTHEW 21:1–5

When they had come near Jerusalem and had reached Bethphage,
at the Mount of Olives, Jesus sent two disciples, saying to them,
"Go into the village ahead of you, and immediately you will find a donkey
tied, and a colt with her; untie them and bring them to me.
If anyone says anything to you, just say this, 'The Lord needs them.'
And he will send them immediately." This took place to fulfill what had
been spoken through the prophet, saying, "Tell the daughter of Zion,
Look, your king is coming to you, humble, and mounted on a donkey,
and on a colt, the foal of a donkey."

—MATTHEW 21:1–5

The people of God in Scripture are often depicted as pilgrims on a journey. Spiritual pilgrimage was not unusual in the days of the Gospel authors. Spiritual journeys of great sages are well documented in the histories of Eastern cultures and religions. It was no different for the Hebrew people of God, as often witnessed when reading the psalms of ascent: the people of God are on an upward journey. Another example of spiritual journeying is the one undertaken by Hannah. Annually, the children of Israel took pilgrimages to Zion. One thing was known about pilgrimages: it required preparation. Stocks of food and water for animals and family alike were imperative. Oh, and don't leave home without the living animals to be offered as sacrifices.

Journeying to a distant temple in search of peace while making great personal sacrifice is found in ancient Eastern epics and religious stories. Jesus on the journey to Jerusalem, the city of peace, epitomises humankind's desire to find ultimate peace in immediate promises. The significant difference in our Lord's story is that he undertook the journey that ended all other futile searches. Unlike the fig tree, which promises much from afar and delivers far from much, Jesus became the destination to end all seeking. He is the destination *and* the journey.

In Holy Week, Jesus himself is on a journey. In the most unassuming way, he will end his pilgrimage by offering himself as the ultimate sacrifice. He will lay a table before enemies for all to come and find feast and fit. It is the most significant journey for all humankind. In the Gospel renditions of the journey, Jesus is both the sacrifice and the satisfying bread. Jesus on the journey to Golgotha is the ultimate incarnation story of hope for humankind on the journey from birth into spiritual rebirth in the life hereafter. It is the ultimate story of our quest for peace. Our journey will be one of hunger and thirst, and those who find him will be satisfied. He is the living water and the bread of life, and we will hunger no more. He is the fulfilment of our life's pursuit. Jesus is our sufficiency for the journey ahead.

QUESTIONS FOR REFLECTION OR DISCUSSION

1. When has peace eluded you?

    _____

    _____

    _____

    _____

    _____

2. What provisions for nourishment have you experienced on your
    daily journey?

    _____

    _____

    _____

    _____

    _____

3. How can you rest in Christ as both the journey and the
    destination?

    _____

    _____

    _____

    _____

PRAYER

*Lord Jesus, send your Spirit to be with us on the journey. Go before us; be
our source and supply. When we are hungry and thirsty on the way, show
us that in the Way we can find satisfying refreshment each and every day.*

Amen.

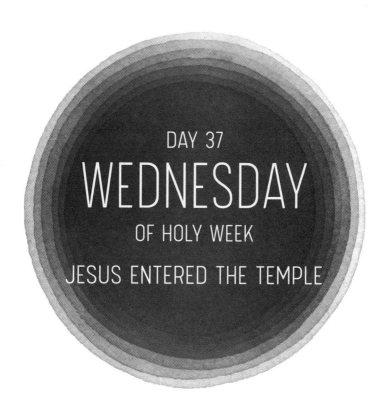

DAY 37

WEDNESDAY

OF HOLY WEEK

JESUS ENTERED THE TEMPLE

SCRIPTURE

MATTHEW 21:12-22

Jesus entered the temple and drove out all who were selling and buying in the temple, and he overturned the tables of the money changers and the seats of those who sold doves. He said to them, "It is written, 'My house will be called a house of prayer;' but you are making it a den of robbers." He left them, went out of the city to Bethany, and spent the night there. In the morning, when he returned to the city, he was hungry. And seeing a fig tree by the side of the road, he went to it and found nothing at all on it but leaves. Then he said to it, "May no fruit ever come from you again!" And the fig tree withered at once.

—*MATTHEW 21:12-13, 17-19*

Matthew portrays Jesus making a singular journey toward the big event. Jesus is on a mission. His work is that of a God-Man figure who shares our humanity and reflects our original, unbroken design of the image of God in us—the hope of glory. In some sense, Matthew appeals to the religio-cultural history of a Moses-like champion who journeys to Pharaoh to call for the liberation of his people. In Jesus we see the hope of what we could be. Jesus is intent on delivering the people who have been yoked by empty religious practices. He wants to free us from that systemic set of oppressive religious expectations. He calls us into intimacy with him. He calls any and all who desire to find rest in him.

Jesus is often heard in Scripture comparing God's way to the religious deception of the day. He emphasises God's way as the better way. He invites hearers to see the fig tree of human religious systems for what it is: a barren system that offers no refreshment on the harsh journey of life. Jesus not only invites the hearer to come and find rest, but he also condemns the religious system from the root, right down to the very elusive fruit that it promises and never delivers. The cursing of the fig tree and the overturning of the temple traders' tables are evidence of Jesus's earnestness to seek and save the lost. These two events don't win him favours or make him popular. Jesus cleanses the temple, forcing all the templegoers to confront the rot in their religion. Then he curses the fruitless fig tree, which symbolises a counterfeit Israel.

QUESTIONS FOR REFLECTION OR DISCUSSION

1. The religio-political leaders think their kingdoms will last forever. How can we be certain our own religion is not empty and fruitless?

_____

_____

_____

_____

2. How can Christians become a shelter, or "house of prayer" for all nations and people groups?

_____

_____

_____

_____

3. How do we know if we are building fruitless kingdoms that will be cursed and wither like the fig tree?

_____

_____

_____

_____

PRAYER

Holy Spirit, fill us with our Lord's love. May our life's fruit be full and abundant in all our practices. As we pursue intimacy with you, cause us to bring forth fruit in keeping with Christlikeness. Oh, that the hungry seeker and the sage alike may find refreshing satisfaction in our fruit and a place at our upright tables. We pray this in Jesus's strong name. Amen.

DAY 38

MAUNDY THURSDAY

DO AS I HAVE DONE

SCRIPTURE

JOHN 13:1-35

Jesus, knowing that the Father had given all things into his hands, and that he had come from God and was going to God, got up from the table, took off his outer robe, and tied a towel around himself. Then he poured water into a basin and began to wash the disciples' feet and to wipe them with the towel that was tied around him. After he had washed their feet, had put on his robe, and had returned to the table, he said to them, "Do you know what I have done to you? You call me Teacher and Lord—and you are right, for that is what I am. So if I, your Lord and Teacher, have washed your feet, you also ought to wash one another's feet. For I have set you an example, that you also should do as I have done to you. By this everyone will know that you are my disciples, if you have love for one another.

—JOHN 13:3-5, 12-15, 35

What I do in service of others does not diminish who I am. Serving others with all that we have within us should be part and parcel of who we are as the people of God. Not far from my home is a museum that my family and I visit each year around the sixteenth of December. The historic site is called The Capture Site. It was the place where Nelson Rolihlahla Mandela was arrested in 1962. He subsequently spent the better part of the next three decades in prison. It is told that the Nobel Laureate, Mr. Mandela, received the name "Nelson" as a student in a little Methodist missionary school in South Africa's Eastern Cape region. The teacher could not pronounce the name Rolihlahla (in Mandela's native Xhosa it means "the one who shakes the branches"), so Nelson was the new name given to the boy at school. He accepted the name, and it became the public image of one of the most recognisable faces in history.

One of my daughters asked as we walked around the museum, "Dad, was Mr. Mandela angry when he was released from prison?"

The other one asked, "What made him choose peace?"

I told them, "Nelson Mandela knew who he was. He understood that you can change the label and the name of the product, but it will do the very work it was designed to do."

Mandela was a great example of a servant leader, but he was not a perfect man. He did say a few profound things, however, one of which was: "There can be no greater gift than giving one's time and energy to help others without expecting anything in return."

Jesus knew who he was, and he knew his purpose. Jesus fully understood that he was not diminished by serving. He was God, *and* he was a servant. The cliched Shakespearean adage comes to mind that a rose by any other name would still smell as sweet. In our service to humanity, may we also not allow the things we do in service to others to lessen who we are. Washing other people's feet sounds dehumanizing and devaluing. It was not so with Jesus. He fully grasped the idea that it was the call to serve. As Paul reminds us in Philippians 2, glory was not something Jesus pursued. Jesus, being God, moved from glory to glory. Even when he washed feet, he was still God. He was God who took on the form of a servant.

Recognising that we are children of God affirmed by the seal of the Holy Spirit, we do not become anything less than what we are in Christ when we serve others. If I had to put this down to hypothetical human currencies, the ten-carat diamond Christ exchanged for my life remains a full ten carats. Whether I am in the world emptying myself serving in the trenches or ruling from a throne, I am everything I am because of the intrinsic worth of Christ in me. *That* is the hope of glory. May we all serve with the full confidence that we remain complete and whole as children of God. We are not made any less as we take on the basin, water, and towel and serve in the world with great humility.

QUESTIONS FOR REFLECTION OR DISCUSSION

1. When have you served someone in humility, and how did your sense of worth increase following that experience?

_____

_____

_____

_____

_____

2. How are you currently serving Jesus? If you feel depleted or diminished, go to the altar and ask Jesus to reveal to you your worth.

_____

_____

_____

_____

_____

_____

PRAYER

Lord Jesus, speak your word and your worth into our lives. Let us have the same mind that you had. You served with no expectation, and you were not disappointed. You were fully aware of your identity and the Creator's image within you. You gave your all, and God the Creator raised you up again, restoring to you your full identity. Let it be done to us in the same way. Raise us up to know that our worth and value are not in what we do but in whose we are and who we are. Amen.

DAY 39
GOOD FRIDAY
AT THAT MOMENT

SCRIPTURE

MATTHEW 27:24-66

Then Jesus cried again with a loud voice and breathed his last.
At that moment the curtain of the temple was torn in two,
from top to bottom. The earth shook, and the rocks were split.

—MATTHEW 27:50-51

As I reflect on the text for today, I find my pastoral mind looking at an alliteration in the outline. The text reveals, first, the *moment of reality*; second, the *monuments of religion*; and third, *movement through relationships*.

Verse 51 begins, "At that moment . . ." In that one moment, the world changes. Moments like this change the past and shape the future. Life happens in moments. It is amazing how a single moment can close yesterday's normal and give way to a new normal. It is amazing now that we speak of the world pre-COVID and post-COVID. It took one moment, and the world switched into the next gear. Hope freezes in the second that things change. I cannot imagine the feeling of helplessness, loneliness, fear, and uncertainty that must have filled the disciples in *that* moment.

We have all had moments when hope lies dead and everything feels irreversible. Not very long ago, all our best knowledge in the sciences and our great trust in our personal security was shattered as the world was covered in the darkness of the rising wave of death that engulfed us all. It was new. "Novel" was the word used to describe the new virus. Every aspect of our lives and systems changed forever. We experienced some of what the disciples must have felt in the moment of Jesus's death—dismay and despair in the face of lives disrupted by death. Helpless. So often we put our faith in our leaders, our systems, our businesses, and our families—until those foundations are shaken and begin to crumble.

Which leads us to our second M-word: *the monuments of religion*. That great historical temple of Israel that stood in Jerusalem as a symbol of God's power and might now stood exposed. The mystery of the inner chamber was revealed. In that moment the God of all the nations removed the intrigue of a historical monument. The temple as a geographical marker began to unveil the fact that worship in this place or that was no longer to be the reality (John 4:21–23). God moved beyond the boundaries of exclusivity and touched the ends of the earth. Love was the new language. God's love now revealed the original intent behind the law: intimacy with God. God is with us. God is for us. God showed up in that moment. When monuments are removed, icons, idols, and religion are replaced with opportunities for intimacy and relationship with God.

Third, *a movement through relationships.* I often hear the voice of the late great preacher and leader from South Africa Mashangu "Harry" Maluleka asking the question, "Can we be a movement again?" All over the world, the Spirit of the Lord is moving. In that moment, when Jesus gave himself up willingly for us and died, the old religion was buried in the tomb. His resurrection gave way to a new intimacy with God. All who believed are given the right to be called children of God. The disciples rediscovered how much they needed one another. With the physical building no longer binding them, they moved out into mission. The disciples discovered the power of meeting together to pray. The moment gave way to a movement. The church moved onto centre stage as the acts of the Holy Spirit through the apostles crafted a new way of living and loving. Panic and pandemonium did not move the movement. Movements are born in the eye of a storm.

Let us take our eyes off the storm for a moment and see the movement that God is mobilising. Behold how the movement morphed but the mission did not die as a result of COVID. Christians were able to point people toward the truth about healing and about God using science that had yet to be discovered to heal and protect people. Behold how we have prayed for one another around the world. See how the church did not cease in our mission to love our neighbours. Whatever the next few weeks, months, or years hold for us as individuals and as families, the church is positioned to move forward in compassion, in courage, and in calmness amid this storm.

QUESTIONS FOR DISCUSSION OR REFLECTION

1. What has been a defining, life-changing moment for you, something that birthed a new way of movement and mission in your life?

    _____

    _____

    _____

    _____

    _____

    _____

    _____

    _____

2. How can Christians trust God's presence in the world-changing moments that turn everything on its head?

    _____

    _____

    _____

    _____

    _____

    _____

    _____

    _____

    _____

PRAYER

The Simple Prayer for Peace, sometimes misattributed to St. Francis of Assisi, dates to approximately 1912.

Lord, make me an instrument of your peace
Where there is hatred, let me sow love
Where there is injury, pardon
Where there is doubt, faith
Where there is despair, hope
Where there is darkness, light
Where there is sadness, joy

O divine Master, grant that I may not so much seek
To be consoled as to console
To be understood as to understand
To be loved as to love

For it is in giving that we receive
It is in pardoning that we are pardoned
It is in dying that we are born to eternal life
Amen

DAY 40
HOLY SATURDAY
A NEW TOMB

SCRIPTURE

JOHN 19:38-42

After these things, Joseph of Arimathea, who was a disciple of Jesus, though a secret one because of his fear of the Jews, asked Pilate to let him take away the body of Jesus. Pilate gave him permission; so he came and removed his body. Nicodemus, who had at first come to Jesus by night, also came, bringing a mixture of myrrh and aloes, weighing about a hundred pounds. They took the body of Jesus and wrapped it with the spices in linen cloths, according to the burial custom of the Jews. Now there was a garden in the place where he was crucified, and in the garden there was a new tomb in which no one had ever been laid. And so, because it was the Jewish day of Preparation, and the tomb was nearby, they laid Jesus there.

—JOHN 19:38-42

Saturday—is it true God lies dead in the tomb? Is it true that death won? Did he say he was finished? That moment of realisation that screams, *The Christ is dead!* Holy Saturday. Jesus's body was still in the tomb. God turned his face. The earth was spiritually darkened. Silence in the grave does not mean silence in all eternal spaces. Stillness in the grave does not mean inactivity in the bowels of hell.

Jesus's body lay dead in the tomb, but the Christ in that moment broke the back of sin and death in hell. Jesus is not simply about Good Friday or Easter Sunday. The prologue and the epilogue are bookends of the volume of Saturday's dialogue. Death is in conference with life itself. He who said, "I am the Way and the Truth and the Life" is in a place that cannot hold him. The incongruency of a grave on earth trying to hold captive the maker of life is just too much. Jesus went beyond the cold stone slab and gave hope to the very bottomless place of hopelessness.

Saturday—that grey day of stillness and mourning—had a different meaning behind the curtaining boulder of burial. Holy Saturday was to the disciples a place of one recurring thought. *Is this it?* How quickly we awake to this day, and the more we think about it, the more we are afraid that the reality of our world points to the unchangeable fact that Jesus is dead. Nothing in our experience changes death. Do we mourn? Do we call out his name? Do we say that name of Jesus followed by, "May he rest in peace"? It cannot be. He was peace, and he was life.

This day in between feels awkward. It is the day when nothing seems to happen. Friday brought confusion; Sunday brought clarity. Friday brought fear; Sunday brought faith. Friday brought opposition; Sunday brought opportunities. Friday brought death; Sunday brought dancing. But what do we do about Saturday? What did the disciples do when the Lord was dead? Dead. Between the agony of Friday and the answers of Sunday, God lay silent on Saturday.

Perhaps you are in the Saturday of your life—a time when it seems God is silent. Know this: God's silence does not mean God is inactive. In the silence of Holy Saturday, God went into hell and broke the power of death. Resurrection power is available to you today. I want to encourage you to release your anxiety to its own grave. God will resurrect peace instead. Release your cares and witness the resurrection of abundant life. Release your time, and he will resurrect eternity within you. The more we hold things without releasing them, the longer Saturday lingers in a sense of despair.

QUESTIONS FOR REFLECTION OR DISCUSSION

1. What do you believe about Holy Saturday?

2. How important is it to reflect on the cost of salvation on Holy Saturday?

3. What calls to you from the silence of Saturday?

PRAYER

On Holy Saturday, peace and confusion merge.
Sing a song of life and love? Or should I sing a dirge?
Where has our Saviour gone?
A pierced side, no broken bone
A picture of death he was, going in
But now earth is restored,
Delivering love triumphant over sin.
Amen.

EASTER SUNDAY

HE HAS BEEN RAISED FROM THE DEAD

SCRIPTURE

MATTHEW 28:1-10; JOHN 20:1-18

After the sabbath, as the first day of the week was dawning, Mary Magdalene and the other Mary went to see the tomb. And suddenly there was a great earthquake; for an angel of the Lord, descending from heaven, came and rolled back the stone and sat on it. His appearance was like lightning, and his clothing white as snow. For fear of him the guards shook and became like dead men. But the angel said to the women, "Do not be afraid; I know that you are looking for Jesus who was crucified. He is not here; for he has been raised, as he said. Come, see the place where he lay. Then go quickly and tell his disciples, 'He has been raised from the dead, and indeed he is going ahead of you to Galilee; there you will see him.' This is my message for you." So they left the tomb quickly with fear and great joy, and ran to tell his disciples.

—*MATTHEW 28:1-8*

They said to her, "Woman, why are you weeping?" She said to them, "They have taken away my Lord, and I do not know where they have laid him." When she had said this, she turned around and saw Jesus standing there, but she did not know that it was Jesus. Jesus said to her, "Mary!" She turned and said to him in Hebrew, "Rabbouni!" (which means Teacher). Jesus said to her, "Do not hold on to me, because I have not yet ascended to the Father. But go to my brothers and say to them, 'I am ascending to my Father and your Father, to my God and your God.'" Mary Magdalene went and announced to the disciples, "I have seen the Lord"; and she told them that he had said these things to her.

—JOHN 20:13-14, 16-18

The world has not changed much when it comes to healing our wounded. Citizens of this world treat trauma with more trauma. It is no surprise that surgery is a wounding for a healing. Vaccines may cause trauma to a few to bring greater relief to more. The earth stands broken. Love and kindness are received with pain and destruction. Many who love deeply arise to be hated by the world. Simply think of the peace proclaimers on the global stage who have been harassed, bullied, stalked, and even killed for their efforts. Jesus reminded his disciples that if the world hated him, it would be no different for those who followed him. Trauma requires deep, significant healing. The cross of Calvary has afforded a full cure.

After we have appreciated the uneasy silence of Saturday, we can fully embrace and love the fullness of the power of Resurrection Sunday. Against all odds, early before the light breaks, the women in the disciples' circle are on their way to the tomb, where God has already called life back from death. The world has new meaning in that moment, and the women are the first to know it. They were the first people of the third day, and now we too are people of the third day. Throughout Scripture, the third day remains a powerful reminder that God always had in mind that a remnant would enjoy the grace and power of the third day. God reveals his grace in multiple third-day events in Scripture.

In Genesis, we are reminded that God provides the redeeming way. It is on the third day that God rescues Isaac from the altar of sacrifice and provides a ram in his place (see Genesis 22:1–14). Again God fore-shadows the redemption plan and shows himself as Immanuel—God with us—in Exodus. On the third day, God reveals himself to God's people on Mount Sinai, reminding them who provides and who keeps promises (see Exodus 19:1–15). In 2 Kings, God heals and restores on the third day (see 2 Kings 20:1–11). The third day will restore us to the house of God. In Esther, God is shown to be the just and true judge over all (see Esther 5).

The third day has long been important for the people of God, and so today we too are the covenant people of the third day. God makes all things new, and we are healed from our trauma. We arise not as those who are simply changed; instead, we emerge out of the grave of trau-ma and silence as a new creation in resurrection. The old is gone; all things have been made new.